Augustus Pugin, Edward James Willson

Examples of Gothic architecture

Selected from various ancient edifices in England

Augustus Pugin, Edward James Willson

Examples of Gothic architecture

Selected from various ancient edifices in England

ISBN/EAN: 9783337278762

Printed in Europe, USA, Canada, Australia, Japan

Cover: Foto ©Andreas Hilbeck / pixelio.de

More available books at **www.hansebooks.com**

EXAMPLES

OF

Gothic Architecture:

SELECTED FROM VARIOUS

ANCIENT EDIFICES IN ENGLAND:

CONSISTING OF

PLANS, ELEVATIONS, SECTIONS, AND PARTS AT LARGE;

CALCULATED TO EXEMPLIFY

THE VARIOUS STYLES,

AND

THE PRACTICAL CONSTRUCTION

OF THIS

ADMIRED CLASS OF ARCHITECTURE:

ACCOMPANIED BY

Historical and Descriptive Accounts.

VOL. I.

BY AUGUSTUS PUGIN.

THE LITERARY PART BY E. J. WILLSON, F.S.A.

Edinburgh
JOHN GRANT
31 GEORGE IV. BRIDGE
1895

PREFACE.

With feelings of the greatest satisfaction, I am at length enabled to present my Work to the Public in a finished state, and I trust that it will be found fully answerable to the conditions announced at the commencement,* and worthy of the flattering encouragement with which it has been carried on. An apology is due to my subscribers for the delay that has taken place in the publication of the letter-press. That delay has been a subject of deep anxiety and uneasiness to me, though beyond my power to avoid, without injury to the work itself; being occasioned principally by the illness and various avocations of the gentleman who had undertaken the literary part of the volume, and who, no less than myself, was extremely desirous of making the "Examples of Gothic Architecture" a truly valuable work, without sparing any pains or expense that might conduce to its perfection.

My thanks are most gratefully offered to the subscribers to my work, and particularly to the many gentlemen professionally engaged in architecture, without whose liberal encouragement and patronage I should not have ventured to undertake the publication.

* The number of Plates has been increased from seventy-two, as originally proposed, to seventy-five, with a corresponding addition to the descriptive part of the subjects.

To Mr. John Le Keux, whose talents are too well known to admit of praise from me, I am much indebted for the satisfactory execution of many of the engravings.

Mr. Willson will accept of my acknowledgments for his friendly and zealous co-operation, not only in the literary department, but also in the choice and arrangement of the subjects, as well as the general plan of the work.

With the assistance of this gentleman, and relying on a continuance of the kind encouragement of my patrons, I intend to commence a second series of "Examples of Gothic Architecture," in a volume of corresponding character to the present. Many sketches and drawings have been prepared for this work, and subscriptions are most respectfully solicited. Every endeavour will be used to render the second series of "Examples" equal, if not superior, to the present; and arrangements made for publishing the letter-press in successive portions at the same periods with the plates, in order to prevent any disappointment at the conclusion of the work.

AUGUSTUS PUGIN.

Remarks
ON
Gothic Architecture
AND
Modern Imitations.

— — —

THE plan adopted for the work entitled "Specimens of Gothic Architecture," has been followed, with little variation, in the volume now presented to the public; which may be regarded as, in fact, a continuation of the "Specimens," although a new title has been thought proper, inasmuch as the "Examples" form an independent work.

In the selection of the subjects, a preference has been given to such as appeared most likely to afford useful lessons to the modern artist; and, with this view, the early varieties of style which distinguish the works of the twelfth and thirteenth centuries have been passed over; the oldest of these "Examples" being dated in the reign of Edward I.* The omission of any *examples* of the *Early Pointed* or *Lancet Style*, will perhaps be censured by some critics, who may insist that a few subjects of that beautiful style ought to have had a place. In extenuation of any such charge, it may

---

* See Plate V. of Merton College, Oxford; and the description at page 2.

be pleaded, that the present work does not offer the display of a complete series of examples in all the successive variations of style; but merely exhibits a selection of such as have appeared best suited for imitation, particularly in domestic architecture, for which the lancet style is peculiarly inconvenient. With this purpose in view, the "Examples" have been chiefly taken from habitable buildings; civil architecture of the Gothic style being much less generally understood than ecclesiastical.

The colleges of the University of Oxford have supplied a large share of subjects, and the excellence of most of those selected will, it is hoped, sufficiently justify their insertion; the works of those venerable and scientific prelates, Wykeham, Waynflete, and Chichelé, being considered by the best judges as pre-eminent models of architectural excellence, wherever they have escaped the injuries of time and barbarous alterations.

The palatial halls of Eltham and Croydon exhibit fine specimens of the open timber roof; especially the former, where the bay-windows are also of exquisite beauty. The stately entrance of Oxborough hall is a superior example of semi-castellated architecture; and a charming variety of rich details will be found in the Plates of East Basham and Thorpland halls, and the rector's house at Great Snoring, in Norfolk. These three mansions are all constructed with brick, and their ornaments show what patient and skilful workmanship may effect, even in the humblest materials; but, without recommending an imitation of such elaborate works, their beautiful forms may be advantageously transferred to stone, which, both in colour and substance, must always hold a superiority over brick.

To the description of the principal subjects, some sketches of their history have been prefixed, in order to give a more comprehensive knowledge of the buildings from which the particular Examples have been taken; and small ground-plans have been introduced for the same purpose.

The above statement will explain the plan and intention of the present work; and some observations on the history of the *Gothic* or *Pointed* style of architecture, and its modern practice, will now be given, in continuation of the introductory essays prefixed to the two volumes of "Specimens."

In one of those essays the study of ancient architecture was compared to that of the dead languages, and some points of analogy were briefly noticed, in order to illustrate the principles of composition.* To pursue a similar idea, the "Examples of Gothic Architecture," as well as the "Specimens," may be aptly compared to collections of personal memoirs, original letters, wills, or other documents of genuine history; whilst books of modern architectural designs rather resemble fictitious narratives, or historical romances. No inferiority of merit is here imputed to such productions, nor is it intended to raise an invidious competition with any works of that description: the only aim is to shew that their merits are of a different order. Here is no claim to invention. Fidelity must constitute the chief value of the work; and, bearing this consideration always in mind, the strictest attention has been paid to the display of every subject exactly as it exists; or, where the original has become imperfect, to ascertain, by a careful examination of those parts which yet remain entire, how much is wanting to restore the whole to a complete state, and so to represent it. Such a task must, of course, be frequently attended with difficulty, and, in certain instances, could not be performed without trusting something to imagination; but no liberty of this sort has been taken where the original authority could be obtained. However, after using all practicable care and diligence, some inaccuracies may perhaps be discovered, and for these the indulgence of the public must be solicited.

The approbation which has been shewn towards the "Specimens" makes it unnecessary to say much on the utility of works of this description. It is only through the medium of accurate prints that a thorough knowledge of the architecture of the middle ages can be obtained; as by the same means the classic orders of Greece and Rome have at length become properly understood.

Very few artists have opportunities of visiting and making an actual examination of any considerable number of the original sub-

---

* Remarks on "Gothic Architecture," in Vol. I. of "Specimens," page xx.

jects; and the variety of invention which these edifices display is so immense, and their details are frequently of such a rich and complicated design, that a patient and experienced hand is necessary to produce a faithful picture. Moreover, a comparison of different subjects is frequently required, in order to discover and elucidate the principles of their design. The want of these aids occasioned the failures of Sir Christopher Wren, Hawksmoor, Kent, and other architects of the two last centuries, in their *Gothic* works. The elements of the style had not then been investigated, their knowledge was limited to superficial observation, and consequently they produced misshapen abortions of taste.—But, it may be asked, are we to be confined to a servile imitation of ancient models? By no means. Such restriction would be absurd. Nevertheless, while so many bald and imperfect designs are continually produced, even in the metropolis, to the disgrace of the modern Gothic school, it must be acknowledged that there is something to be learned, before our works shall bear a comparison with those of our forefathers. The trusting too much to invention, without sufficient science, has produced an infinity of contemptible designs. The *Gothic Architecture* of Batty Langley is universally condemned, and very justly;* but other artists ought to take a part in his shame; for, long since the unlucky publication of his "Five Gothic Orders," some inventions, scarcely less barbarous, have been put forth by certain architects, who must afterwards have blushed at their early productions. Unfortunately, some of these wretched works, after being discarded from the

---

* See "Gothic Architecture improved by Rules and Proportions, in many grand Designs of Columns, &c. &c. by B. and T. Langley. To which is added, an Historical Dissertation on Gothic Architecture," in 4to. The number of plates is sixty-two; all produced by the brothers, Batty and Thomas Langley, and dated in the years 1741, 1742. The prefatory dissertation is signed with the initials B. L., and occupies seven pages. In it the author states, that he had assiduously employed himself for upwards of twenty years in recovering the rules of our ancient architecture, which had been lost for many centuries, in order to restore and publish them for the good of posterity, &c. Such an instance of perverted ingenuity was perhaps never exhibited by any other person; for it is hardly conceivable, that a man should study the ancient buildings of his own country for twenty years, and then produce nothing but a parcel of strange inventions, totally unlike what

library, have found their way into the workshop, or the mechanic's lodging, and there they may continue to disseminate false taste, where it is not likely to be soon corrected.*

Since the revival of the Gothic style, in the reign of George III., no abatement of public favour towards this beautiful species of architecture has been hitherto manifested: on the contrary, a great number of country-seats, for the residence of the nobility and gentry, has been raised within the last few years, in imitation of castles, abbeys, and mansions of the fifteenth and sixteenth centuries. A prodigious sum has been expended in the repair and embellishment of the royal castle of Windsor. Some of the principal colleges at Oxford have been repaired with a commendable attention to their original style, and many grievous injuries inflicted on those venerable edifices have been amended, though not with uniform correctness. The University of Cambridge has received still greater improvements, by the erection of some magnificent buildings, mostly in the style of the fifteenth century. Many new parochial churches and chapels have been erected, in order to accommodate the increased population of the metropolis, and of some provincial towns, in professed imitation of our old ecclesiastical architecture. The repair of several cathedrals has been prosecuted with becoming liberality, and a strictness of architectural propriety heretofore unknown. Amongst these works the chief place must doubtless be given to the restoration of the choir of York Minster, after its destruction by an incendiary, mad with fanaticism. We may justly expect to see this superb structure

had ever been practised. The same *architect* also published, besides his *opus magnum*, "The Builder's Director or Bench-Mate, being a Pocket Treasury of the Grecian, Roman, and Gothic Orders of Architecture;" with several other works of a small size. His *Gothic* designs are execrable; but his manner of displaying the details of Italian architecture was very neat and useful.

* I very lately saw a workman of good talents diligently employed in modelling from a most barbarous design,—a genuine specimen of the *Langleian Gothic* school, though published by a celebrated architect. This ingenious man had been favoured with the use of the book by his master, who had much better have committed it to the fire.

renovated in all its former beauty, since public munificence has provided ample funds for the work. Winchester and Peterborough cathedrals, the collegiate church of Beverley, and some other principal churches, have received very considerable reparations; and many of our ancient parochial churches have participated in the general improvement.*

This extensive revival of Gothic Architecture has excited a more attentive study of its proportions and peculiarities, and knowledge has in its turn diffused a better taste. Not only are such gross anomalies as the chapel of Lincoln's Inn, and the towers of Westminster Abbey, condemned as barbarous, and unworthy of true genius; but even the imperfect efforts of some later architects, who professed to admire and follow the style which Inigo Jones and Sir Christopher Wren avowedly despised and neglected,—even these are now censured, and have their faults exposed. When the cathedrals of Hereford, Durham, Salisbury, and Lichfield, were altered agreeably to the taste of the late Mr. James Wyatt, only a few professed antiquaries dared to remonstrate. Mr. Gough, Sir Henry Englefield, Dr. Milner, and John Carter, openly censured the gross violations of antiquity committed in those churches;† but their interference was generally treated with ridicule, or resented with indignation. Salisbury and Lichfield were thought to be much improved by the demolition of their altar-screens, the throwing open of the smaller chantries, and the removal of the ancient tombs from the graves to which they belonged, in order to range them in rank and file. These barbarisms were praised and admired, because the public mind was ignorant on the subject.

* The state of the greater number of country churches, however, is very deplorable. They are either neglected, and become unfit for use, from the damp and dirty state into which they have gradually fallen; or are disfigured and mutilated by tasteless and penurious attempts at repair. It is hard to say which of these modes of destruction is the worst; but, between the two, many noble monuments of the taste and piety of past ages, which will never be replaced, are daily sinking into ruin.

† See the "Gentleman's Magazine" for 1789, 1790, 1796, &c.—Dr. Milner published "A Dissertation on the Modern Style of altering Ancient Cathedrals." Second edition, 4to, 1811.

Fortunately, a partial check was put to the progress of innovation, and Durham Cathedral was saved from the completion of its intended improvements. The magnificent rere-dos of the high altar, the episcopal throne, the western chapel, called the "Galilee," and the "Nine Altars" at the east end, were left untouched; but the chapter-house, which had no equal in its peculiar style, was sacrificed for the erection of a common square parlour; and the pencil of the indefatigable John Carter has preserved all that is left to posterity of that most curious edifice. Such havoc could not be committed with impunity in the present day, or at least it would soon become a subject of general and severe animadversion;* for the study of ancient architecture is not now confined to the mere antiquary, but has become almost a part of polite education, and no architect can make any creditable pretensions to professional knowledge without an intimate acquaintance with the varieties of the Gothic style.

The revival of Gothic architecture seems almost peculiar to this country; scarcely any thing having been done on the continent in the construction of modern buildings after this manner, and but little in the investigation of ancient monuments. This backwardness of taste in our neighbours is mortifying to the English student; as undoubtedly a great fund of curious information, relative to the practice of architecture during the middle ages, will be brought forth whenever the study of the Gothic style shall become general on the continent. One important fact has been abundantly evinced; viz., that there are no solid grounds for the pretensions advanced by certain writers to the pointed arch as our national invention, in consequence of which they presumed to apply the denomination of "*English Architecture*" to the cathedrals and other edifices in which it prevails. The origin of the pointed arch, after the most earnest and active researches, still remains a very obscure

* This may be inferred from the excitement shewn on the proposed removal of the ancient rood-loft, now used for the organ, in York Minster. Those gentlemen who are advocates of that measure, would do well to peruse the "Dissertation" referred to in the last note.

question; but the period of its becoming a prominent feature in the architecture of Europe seems to have been incontrovertibly ascertained; and all the variations of style successively prevalent in England, from the time of its introduction to the latest use of the pointed arch, have been minutely traced, and their respective ages discovered by the evidence of historical records, or satisfactory analogy. Whether the architects of France or Germany preceded their English brethren in the march of invention, or not, must remain unsettled till the monuments of those countries shall have been thoroughly investigated, and their proportions and details exemplified by geometrical delineations; for the verbal descriptions of travellers are of very little practical use, and perspective views can seldom be relied upon,—critical accuracy in such productions being too commonly regarded of small importance in comparison with a pleasing effect.

The ancient architecture of Normandy has undergone a tolerably accurate examination, and some of its principal monuments have been made familiar to the English architect, through the exertions of his own countryman.* This commencement will, it is hoped, stimulate the French nation to undertake the task of investigation on a liberal and extended scale. The Society of Antiquaries of Normandy have published a few essays, illustrative of the history of some early buildings in that province,† but the study of Gothic architecture in France is still in its infancy, and may be dated half

* "Account of a Tour in Normandy," by Dawson Turner, Esq. F.R.S. 2 vols. 8vo, 1820.
"The Architectural Antiquities of Normandy," by J. S. Cotman. Folio, 1820.
"Specimens of the Architectural Antiquities of Normandy," by Augustus Pugin, Architect. 4to, 1828.
The latter work is on a similar plan to the English "Specimens of Gothic Architecture." It contains eighty plates, in which are displayed some edifices of great interest to the architectural student: particularly the two abbeys erected at Caen by William the Conqueror and his Queen Matilda, the cathedral of Bayeux, and the exquisite church of St. Ouen at Rouen, together with some beautiful specimens of domestic architecture, of a style quite unlike any thing in England.
† "Mémoires de la Société des Antiquaires de la Normandie," 8vo, 1824, 1825, 1826, &c.

a century later than in England. Nor has the inquiry been extensively prosecuted in Germany, where, however, some highly interesting facts have been brought to light, particularly in the discovery of several ancient and original designs for Gothic edifices of great splendour,* whereas scarcely any thing of the kind has been found in England of earlier date than the reign of Queen Elizabeth, although many such drawings were undoubtedly preserved in the libraries of the cathedrals, monasteries, and colleges, previous to the ravages of the sixteenth century.†

The comparison of the Gothic style, as seen in the cathedrals and other principal edifices of the continent, with the monuments of it in our own country, would furnish matter for a very interesting inquiry. But as even a hasty discussion of such an extensive subject would exceed the limits of this essay, it shall for the present be left untouched, and a conclusion be put to these Remarks on Gothic Architecture.‡

EDWARD JAMES WILLSON.

---

* Dr. George Mollers, of Darmstadt, has published several scientific works on the architecture of the middle ages in Germany. An essay on the origin and progress of Gothic architecture, prefixed to one of his works, has been translated from the German, and published in the English language, by Messrs. Priestley and Weale, 1824. See also Boisserée on the Cathedral of Cologne, &c. The "Architectural Notes on German Churches," by Professor Whewell, [8vo, Cambridge, 1830] contain some valuable information ; but the system of technical phraseology adopted by the learned author is defective, and the defence of the terms " Early English," " Decorated English," &c. is quite untenable.

† An original design for the bell-tower of King's College, Cambridge, has been engraved for Lysons's " Magna Britannia," vol. ii. p. 116 ; Pl. XXX.

‡ An intelligent writer in the "Quarterly Review" has observed, that " we may safely use the term *Gothic*, incorrect as it sounds to the critical ear, without prejudice to the cause of truth : knowing that it was formed according to an erroneous hypothesis, it ceases to convey any erroneous idea, and becomes correct by its conventional application. The toleration of etymological inaccuracy, by which a derivative becomes a radical, and obtains a new primitive meaning, is one of the most ordinary processes of the formation of language."—Vol. xxv. p. 139. " The phrase *Gothic Architecture* conveys no reproach ; does

not necessarily imply any hypothetical belief; and as it seems confined, by universal consent, to that style which, however otherwise varied, is ever characterised by the pointed arch, we see no reason why the first efforts of the development of this style should not be called *Early Gothic.*"—*British Critic*, No iv. p. 375. (Published in July 1826.) The futility of the appellation of *English Architecture* was ably exposed in the above periodical works; see also the "Remarks" prefixed to vol. ii. of "Specimens of Gothic Architecture." The novel term of "*Christian Architecture*" has been proposed by Mr. Britton, which, "as a generic term," he apprehends, "will be not only unobjectionable, but will be appropriate, precise, and correct."—[Architectural Antiquities, vol. v. p. 31.] This appellation would imply too much, since Christianity had been established in all the civilised parts of Europe for several ages before the *Gothic* or *Pointed* style appeared; nor was it ever received in the chief city of the Christian world, Rome. If a term were to be borrowed from religion, it might be more properly denominated "*Catholic Architecture*," inasmuch as the sublimest productions of this style were originally dedicated to the solemnities of the Catholic liturgy; and, on the other hand, its destruction immediately followed the subversion of Catholicity. But it is too late now to expect that the accustomed phraseology should be superseded by any new term, excepting only so far as may relate to some particular details or varieties of style.

EXAMPLES

OF

Gothic Architecture.

LIST OF SUBJECTS AND PLATES CONTAINED IN THE WORK.

The Figures, from 1 to 73, mark the Numerical Arrangement of the Plates, for binding, &c.

1. Title Page—MAGDALEN COLLEGE, Oxford—Principal Entrance.

OXFORD—MERTON COLLEGE.

2.   Compartment of the Chapel.
3.   Doorway to North Transept.
4.   Specimens of Ancient Stained Glass.
5.   Compartment of the Chancel.

———— BALLIOL COLLEGE.

6.   Oriel Window.
7.   Section and Details of ditto.

———— NEW COLLEGE.

8.   Part of the Cloisters.
9.   Gable and Details of the Chapel.

———— ALL SOULS COLLEGE.

10.   Entrance Tower.
11.   Vaulted Roof of a Passage leading to the Chapel.
12.   Compartment of the Chapel.
13.   Back of the Stalls in the Chapel.

OXFORD—St. John's College.

14.	Entrance Tower.
15.	Vaulted Roof of a Passage leading to the Garden.
16.	Tracery on the Great Doors.

—— Magdalen College.

17.	Western Porch of the Chapel.
18.	Section and Details of ditto.
19.	Details of Ornaments of ditto.
20.	Compartment and Details of the Chapel.
21.	Chimney-head and Turret of ditto.
22.	Oriel Window in the West Front.
23, 24.	Elevations of the Inward and Outward Fronts of the Entrance Tower (Double Plate).
25.	Ornamental Details of the Entrance Tower.
26.	Details of Mouldings, &c. &c.

—— Brazennose College.

27.	Outward Front of the Entrance Tower.

—— St. Peter's Church.

28.	South Porch.
29.	Sections and Plan of ditto.

—— St. Mary's Church.

30.	Compartment and Details of the Nave.
31.	Compartment and Details of the Chancel.
32.	Stone Stalls in the Chancel.

LONDON—St. Katharine's, Tower Hill.

33.	Canopy of a Stall.

HERTS—St. Alban's Abbey.

34.	Two Doors to Chapel.

SURREY—Beddington Church.

35.	Screen in the Chancel.
36.	Tomb of Sir Richard Carew.

SURREY—BEDDINGTON MANOR HOUSE.
37.   Lock on the Hall Door.

——— ARCHIEPISCOPAL PALACE, at Croydon.
38.   Transverse Section and Details of the Hall.
39.   Compartment and Section of ditto.
40.   Bay Window in the Guard Room.

KENT—ELTHAM PALACE.
41.   Groined Roof of a Bay Window.
42.   Sections, &c. of ditto.
43.   Windows and Details, &c. ditto.
44, 45.   Transverse Section and Plan of the Hall (Double Plate).
46.   North Door.
47.   Pendent and Details of the Roof of ditto.

NORFOLK—OLD WALSINGHAM CHURCH.
48.   Carved Oak Seat.

——— NEW WALSINGHAM CHURCH.
49.   Oak Ceiling.

——— FAKENHAM CHURCH.
50.   Western Door.
51.   Details of a Niche.

——— OXBURGH HALL.
52.   Outward Front of the Entrance Tower.
53.   Turret and Details of ditto.
54.   Section and Plans of ditto.
55.   Inward Front and Plans of ditto.
56.   Details of a Window, and other Parts of ditto.

——— WOLTERTON MANOR-HOUSE, at East Barsham.
57.   South Front and Plan.
58.   Outward Front of the Entrance Tower.
59.   Inward Front of ditto.

NORFOLK—WOLTERTON MANOR-HOUSE, at East Barsham.

- 60. Front of the Porch, with Details.
- 61. Bay Window of the Hall.
- 62. Elevation and Section of a Tower.
- 63. Elevations and Plans of Two Turrets.
- 64. Ornamental Details of the Entrance Tower.
- 65. Stack of Chimneys, with Plan of ditto.
- 66. Details of Ornaments to ditto.
- 67. ——— Mouldings and Ornaments.
- 68. ——— Windows, Door, &c.

——— THORPLAND HALL.

- 69. Front Elevation.
- 70. Gable End and Chimneys.
- 71. Elevation, Section, &c. of the Porch.

——— PARSONAGE HOUSE, Great Snoring.

- 72. South Front, with Details.
- 73. Ornamental Details of ditto.

Examples

OF

Gothic Architecture.

MERTON COLLEGE, OXFORD.
Founded A.D. 1264.

THE Chapel, or, to speak more properly, the *Church*, attached to Merton College, originally belonged to the parish of St. John the Baptist, and was appropriated to the college in the year 1292, by Oliver Sutton, Bishop of Lincoln, to whose diocese Oxford then appertained : the parishioners, however, did not lose their right to the church, which still continues to be parochial as well as collegiate.*

This is an edifice of very solemn and venerable appearance. It consists of a chancel, or choir, with a transept at the west end, and a tower rising from the intersection; to which only a nave is wanting to complete the plan in form of a cross.† The large arch under the west side of the tower shews that the builders intended to construct a nave, and two smaller arches at the sides

---

* The chapel of Jesus College, Cambridge, was originally a parochial church; afterwards it was appropriated to a convent of nuns; and lastly became attached to the college. It is built in form of a cross, but is much inferior in architectural beauty to Merton Chapel, though more complete in plan.

† The cathedral church of Bristol, formerly belonging to an abbey, exactly resembles Merton chapel in its plan; nor is it known whether the nave was ever erected or not.

indicate also that there were to be aisles, though the choir and transept have not those appendages. This part of the church was probably never completed; at least, there are no remains now standing, nor has any record concerning it been discovered.* The choir was probably erected soon after the college had gained possession of the church, as its architecture corresponds to that of other edifices of the age of Edward I.† The transept appears to be of later date by a century or more; but the general proportions of the whole correspond so well, that the dissimilarity of details produces no discordant effect. The learned antiquary, Anthony à Wood, discovered a record of the dedication of this church in the year 1424, at which time the whole was probably finished.

Two of the wardens of Merton College were celebrated for their skill in architecture, and both are supposed to have assisted in building the church. First, William Rede, who began the library in 1376, and also erected Amberley Castle in Sussex, after he had become Bishop of Chichester, in 1396. Second, Thomas Rodburne, who was afterwards Bishop of St. David's, where he died in 1442. This prelate erected the northern entrance-tower of the college, about the year 1416; and the tower of the church has also been attributed to him, but this is merely matter of conjecture.‡

PLATE I. COMPARTMENT ON THE EAST SIDE OF THE NORTH TRANSEPT.

The transept projects beyond the south side of the choir in two compartments, or bays, and two on the north, one of which is here represented.

---

* The west end would probably have extended to the ground on which Corpus Christi College has since been erected.

† Many of the details bear a close resemblance to those of the nave of York Minster, though on a much smaller scale. The first stone of that magnificent structure was laid in the year 1291; but the whole was not finished in less than 40 years.

‡ We learn from Anthony à Wood, that when the five bells were re-cast into eight, in the year 1657, the name of Dr. Henry Abendon was found inscribed upon the tenor bell. He was elected warden in 1421; and these bells had been put up whilst he held that office, soon after the tower was built. It is remarkable, that the pinnacles and perforated battlements of Merton tower so nearly resemble those of the great tower of Magdalene College, that they would both seem of the same date, were there not recorded evidence to the contrary. Perhaps the design for the latter had been drawn long before its erection. The first stone of Magdalene tower was laid on the 9th of August, 1492; and it was scarcely finished in the year 1509, as appears by the registers cited in Dr. Chandler's Life of the Founder of Magdalene College, William of Waynflete, Bishop of Winchester.

No. 1. Elevation of the whole, with the double buttress at the angle.
No. 2. Section taken through the window, and buttress.
No. 3. Details of a pinnacle on a larger scale.
No. 4. Sections of the jamb, mullion, and sill of the window, shewing the curves of all their mouldings.

PLATE II. DOORWAY TO NORTH TRANSEPT.

The design of this door-case is worthy of notice; the proportions being well adjusted, and the details very elaborately moulded. Part of the elevation appears to have been cut off, to give room for sections of the various mouldings, which will be best explained by the engraving.

PLATE III. SPECIMENS OF STAINED GLASS IN THE WINDOWS OF MERTON CHAPEL.

The side-windows of the choir retain much of their original glazing, which is particularly valuable, as affording specimens of a very early style of stained glass, as well as for its elegance of design. The principal lights contain figures of saints, of small proportion, depicted in colours, and standing in stalls or tabernacles. Above and below these, the glass is disposed in various geometrical lines, diapered over with slender branches and foliage. A border of rich colours, composed of leaves and heraldic figures, surrounds each light; and various roundels and small pieces of colour are intermingled with the white glass. To shew some specimens of this curious glazing more perfectly, this Plate has been coloured after the original. The small portrait in a circle seems to represent Queen Eleanor, the beloved wife of Edward I., to whose memory he erected the celebrated Crosses at Waltham and other places.* This portrait certainly resembles the statues of the queen, and the inference is confirmed by the armorial badge of Castile repeated in the borders of the windows.

PLATE IV. EXTERIOR COMPARTMENT ON THE NORTH SIDE OF THE CHANCEL.

The chancel, or rather the *choir*, has seven windows on each side, all of the same general proportions, but of different patterns in the tracery of the heads.

* Queen Eleanor was suddenly taken ill whilst proceeding with the king, who was going on an expedition against the Scots, and died at Harby, an obscure hamlet about five miles from Lincoln, but on the borders of Nottinghamshire, A.D. 1290. Some small parts of Merton choir resemble the queen's crosses, particularly in the inside near to the altar, where a clumsy monument for Sir Henry Saville has destroyed a part of the elegant stone stalls in the south wall.

This Plate shews one complete bay, or compartment, on the north side, in an external elevation, together with a perpendicular section, and several parts at large.*

A comparison of this Plate with No. 2 will shew the difference of style between the choir and transept. In the choir the design appears more bold and vigorous, whilst the later example shews a more delicate taste in the moulded details. The cornice under the parapet of the choir is most curiously sculptured.

BALLIOL COLLEGE, OXFORD.
Founded A.D. 1282.

THE ancient buildings of this college have been so much mutilated, that very few parts remain sufficiently perfect to serve as architectural models. The entrance-tower and about one half of the quadrangle were erected in the fifteenth century, and were originally of elegant architecture; but the beauty of this court is much injured by the eastern apartments, which were rebuilt about a century ago, in the modern style, forming a huge, heavy, and clumsy pile.

Fortunately this exquisite window has escaped with little injury.† It belongs to a chamber in the master's lodgings, at the upper end of the hall, on the north side of the quadrangle. The arms sculptured on the corbels, or pendents, shew it to have been erected by William Grey, Bishop of Ely,‡ and sometime Lord Treasurer of England. This prelate was of the noble family of the Lords Grey of Codnor, and is known to have contributed to the buildings of this college, where he commenced his education.

So rich and beautiful an example of the oriel, or bay-window, can rarely be seen.§ The proportions are good, and the delicacy of its sculptured ornaments give to the exterior an air of Corinthian richness.

---

* See "Specimens of Gothic Architecture," vol. i. Plates 73, 75, and vol. ii. Plates 18, 26, and 39, for some details of other parts.
† The plain embattled parapet is of modern work.
‡ From 1454 to 1478.
§ At Lincoln College is another window of the same style, and nearly alike to this in most of the details.

Plate I. shews the external elevation, with half the plan, and half of the tracery on the lower parts.

Plate II. gives a perpendicular section, shewing the projection of the window from the wall, its elevation above the floor of the chamber, and the mouldings of the inner arch ; with some details which need no explanation.

NEW COLLEGE, OXFORD.
Founded A.D. 1379.

THE founder of this college, William of Wykeham, Bishop of Winchester, was the most celebrated person of his age for the practice of architecture, of which he left some most noble monuments.* He was no less eminent for his munificent foundations for the encouragement of piety and learning, of which this college was the chief. Its buildings undoubtedly exceeded those of any college previously erected, and served as models for some others of later institution. The foundation was laid in 1380, and the society made their solemn entrance into the new *College of St. Mary* in 1386 ; but some of the buildings were finished several years later. Unfortunately, successive modern additions and alterations, made with more regard to convenience than taste, have obliterated the original style of the greater part of the ancient buildings. The cloisters remain entire, as they were finished A.D. 1400, when they were consecrated as a cemetery for the deceased members of the college. The architecture of these cloisters is plain, but of a very good style ; they surround a quadrangular area, and are roofed with timber, framed in arched ribs.

Plate I. shews two compartments, with a plan and section.

The chapel is a noble and finely-proportioned structure, on which the pious founder spared no expense to render it worthy of its sacred purpose. It suffered considerable injury during the civil war, and was much disfigured by the repairs that were afterwards made, without attention to the proper style of architecture. But about forty years since, a complete restoration of its pristine beauty was determined upon by the collegiate body, who called in

---

* Particularly the castles of Windsor and Queenborough ; the nave of Winchester Cathedral, in which he lies buried within a beautiful chantry ; and two colleges of his own endowment, this at Oxford, and another at Winchester.

the professional aid of the most celebrated architect of the day for effecting this delicate task.*

A new roof was then erected; the interior of the chapel was cleared of some modern furniture of incongruous style, and the whole repaired and fitted up in the manner in which it now appears. Still, however brilliant may be the general effect, the admirers of ancient art cannot but lament the many violations of that pure style which characterises the architecture of Wykeham.

A few ornamental parts have been here selected from the western gable of the chapel; see Plate II. These seem to require no further description than the references given with the different figures on the Plate.

ALL SOULS COLLEGE, OXFORD.

Founded A.D. 1437.

THE noble example of William of Wykeham was followed with equal liberality by Henry Chichelé, Archbishop of Canterbury, in the foundation of All Souls College.† This prelate was far advanced in years when he commenced his college: he had been personally acquainted with Wykeham, and a partaker of his bounty in his youth, having been educated at Winchester and New College.

The foundation was laid February 10, 1437, and the warden and fellows entered the new buildings in 1442, in which year the chapel was consecrated, although the whole structure of the college was not complete till 1444.

---

* The late Mr. James Wyatt, who about the same time made great repairs and alterations in the cathedrals of Salisbury, Hereford, and Lichfield; and afterwards at Durham.

† He was born about the year 1362, and, after completing his studies, passed through various ecclesiastical preferments with great credit, and was made Bishop of St. David's in 1407; from whence he was advanced to the metropolitan chair of Canterbury in 1414. His architectural works, and liberal endowments for learning and charity, were scarcely inferior to those of the illustrious Wykeham. The cathedral of Canterbury was much adorned by him; he also founded a library there; he contributed to the building of Rochester bridge, and of the church at Croydon, in Surrey. The palace at Lambeth was much enlarged and beautified by him. At Higham Ferrars, co. Northampton, the place of his birth, the archbishop built and endowed a college, attached to the parochial church. And at Oxford, he erected a small college for scholars of the monastic order of Cistercians, before his foundation of All Souls College. This eminent prelate died in the year 1443, and is buried under a sumptuous monument in Canterbury Cathedral.

John Druell, Archdeacon of Exeter, and Roger Keyes, both fellows of the college, were employed by the founder to conduct the work, of which the expenses, for building only, amounted to 4156*l.* 5*s.* 3¼*d.** The plan of New College seems to have been adopted at All Souls, in regard to the forms and arrangement of the principal apartments; though the architects judiciously attended to the circumstances of a different site, and followed the style of ornament which was fashionable in their own day.

Plate I. Gateway of All Souls College.

This entrance-tower deserves our admiration, both for its lofty and elegant proportions, as well as for the neatness and delicacy of its ornaments. It belongs to the western quadrangle of the ancient buildings, of which the north side is formed by the hall and chapel. The statues in the two lower niches of the outward front represent King Henry VI., the reigning sovereign of that time, and the founder, Archbishop Chichelé. In the larger niche, above these, are sculptures intended to represent angels praying for the relief of human souls, of which a group is seen beneath, involved in the flames of purgatory. These sculptures bore an allusion to one object of the founder's institute, that of prayer for the faithful departed.

The inward front of the tower is of a plainer character than that which faces the High Street, but is designed in regular accordance with it. See No. 2 on the Plate.

Plate II. Compartment of the Chapel, All Souls College.

An elevation of a single bay, or compartment, of the chapel is shewn in this Plate, together with a section made through one pier. Attached to this is seen part of one of the trusses of the roof, which is constructed of oak, wrought in an ornamental fashion, and decorated with mouldings and carved knots. The windows exhibit rather early examples of the obtusely-pointed arch.† The buttresses, pinnacles, and detail of mouldings, are all designed with great neatness and precision. Several of the mouldings are here shewn in sections of an enlarged scale.

---

* A sum equivalent to 100,000*l.* of modern money; or perhaps more.

† This observation applies only to windows. The flat arch was used much earlier in gateways, where its shape was found more convenient than the high-pointed arch.

PLATE III. GROINED CEILING OF A PASSAGE LEADING TO THE CHAPEL.

This example of what is frequently termed a fan-groined vault, is a beautiful specimen of the skill and taste of the masons of the fifteenth century in a difficult branch of architecture. Were a ceiling of such an elaborate design wanted in a modern building, it would be executed in wood and plaster,—materials which require but little, comparatively, of either labour or science; but to construct such a roof of stone, an accurate knowledge of geometrical principles is necessary, and the combination of these scientific requisites with such an elaborate pattern of ornament forms no easy task. The various lines of the arched ribs, the joints of the masonry, and the mouldings, are so fully delineated in the Plate as to make any verbal explanation seem unnecessary.

PLATE IV. TRACERY AT THE BACK OF THE STALLS IN THE CHAPEL.

The choir of All Souls Chapel has suffered so many alterations, at times when every thing in architecture differing from the *Five Orders* was looked upon as unworthy of study or imitation, that the original style is intermingled with ornaments of most discordant taste.* This example is part of the ancient design, and shews a very elegant specimen of the curved gable. The details are simple and appropriate, sufficiently bold and rich, without being crowded.

ST. JOHN'S COLLEGE, OXFORD.
Founded A.D. 1555.

THE buildings of St. John's College are partly of an earlier date than the present establishment, which was founded in the reign of Queen Mary, by Sir Thomas White, a wealthy merchant and alderman of London, who expended vast sums in public charity.

The entrance-tower, and other buildings of the first quadrangle, were erected by Archbishop Chichelé, who founded here a college for scholars of

---

* Notwithstanding these architectural anomalies, the harmonious disposition of rich but sober colour, heightened by gilding, spreads a charm through the interior of this chapel, which has been generally felt.

the Cistercian order of monks, which fell under the acts of Henry VIII. for the dissolution of monasteries. The deserted buildings were purchased of the college of Christ Church, to which St. Bernard's College had been granted, and were appropriated by Sir Thomas White to his new establishment, which dates its foundation from the year 1555.

The entrance bears so great a resemblance to that of All Souls College, that we may attribute them with great probability to the same architect. The general outline of St. John's tower has more simplicity, its height being divided into only three stories, whilst in that of All Souls there are four. The principal arch has a greater depth and richness of mouldings, and the projection of the bay-window immediately over the arch relieves a certain flatness in the centre, perceptible at All Souls. Both, however, are beautiful examples of the same style, and their variations only make them more interesting. The two vacant niches were probably intended for statues of the king and the founder, as at All Souls: that in the upper story is thought to represent St. Bernard, the patron saint of the monastic college.

PLATE I. No. 1. Elevation of the external front.
No. 2. Perpendicular section.
No. 3. Plan of the gateway, shewing the lines of the arched roof.

PLATE II. VAULTED ROOF IN ST. JOHN'S COLLEGE.

This example of a fretted roof may be compared with one in a preceding Plate, taken from All Souls College. They are of nearly similar style. In this, however, we find one species of ornament of a later fashion, in the pendent spandrils: an invention of the last architects of the Gothic style, which they in some instances exhibited with marvellous boldness and ingenuity.*

The various delineations of this curious vault will, it is hoped, display

---

* The royal chapels at Windsor and Westminster shew the finest examples in England of pendents in their vaulted roofs. At Oxford, the Divinity School and the choir of Christ Church Cathedral may be noticed for similar enrichments. There are some examples in France of still more extraordinary construction, in which pendent groins of great depth descend from the roofs to which they are attached. This roof at St. John's College has been attributed to Inigo Jones, who was employed by Archbishop Laud, in the reign of Charles I., to erect the library and other parts of the inner quadrangle.

its construction and ornaments so fully, as to make the whole easily understood: no farther description will therefore be added to what has been said above.

PLATE III. No. 1. In the upper part of this Plate will be found an elevation of the gates of St. John's College, with an enlarged delineation of the tracery on one of the folding-doors, and also a section of the mouldings which divide the tracery into panels.

No. 2. The subjects of the lower half of the Plate are taken from Merton College Chapel: being parts of the ancient stalls. These are apparently of coeval date with the transept, their style being evidently much later than that of the choir.*

MAGDALEN COLLEGE, OXFORD.

Founded A.D. 1457.

THE ancient buildings of Magdalen College exhibit some very fine examples of the architecture of the fifteenth century, so happily placed in a spacious and open situation, that they are shewn in various points of view with peculiar advantage. These venerable edifices have not escaped without much injury, and have even been threatened with almost total demolition, in order to make room for modern plans, of entirely different style: however, the principal portions of this College remain much more perfect than those of New College and All Souls; and it is hoped that the learned body who possess these beautiful monuments of their founder's taste, will preserve them, as much as possible, in their original state.

The College of St. Mary Magdalen was founded in the year 1457, by William of Waynflete, Bishop of Winchester, upon the site of an ancient hospital, dedicated to St. John the Baptist, which was previously resigned by the master and brethren, and dissolved, or rather incorporated with the

* The choir of Merton Chapel was fitted up at the beginning of the last century with new stalls and other furniture, which are decorated with cornices and pilasters of the Corinthian order. Some ancient stalls are preserved in the transept, from which the present subject has been drawn.

college.* A considerable period elapsed, after its legal establishment, during which the members of the college were lodged in the old buildings of St. John's hospital; the exertions of the founder being impeded by the troubled state of the kingdom, which was then harassed by the contending factions of the rival houses of York and Lancaster. It was not until 1474, that a regular set of collegiate buildings was commenced. On the 5th of May in that year the first stone was laid with due solemnity, in the place where the high altar of the chapel was to be erected. "We find Waynflete contracting with William Orchyerd, the principal mason, in 1475, 1478, and the following year, for finishing the tower over the gateway with a pyramid sixteen feet high above the level of the gutter; for crowning the walls of the chapel and hall with niched battlements; for a coping to these and the library; for completing the chambers, cloisters, and other imperfect portions of the fabric; and for fashioning the great window of the chapel, with the windows of the chambers, after the model of All Souls."† The distribution of the principal buildings was made in a great measure on a plan similar to those of New College and All Souls. The entrance to the principal court or quadrangle faces the west, and is surmounted by a tower. The quadrangle is surrounded by cloisters, over which is a floor of chambers, on three sides, the fourth being backed by the hall and chapel, which form together one long, lofty range of building, in the external view. The chapel consists of a choir without aisles, and of a short nave of corresponding height, but having an aisle added to its breadth on each side. These aisles are of the same height as the nave, and are

* A previous step to the foundation of the college was made A.D. 1448, when Bishop Waynflete obtained license of Henry VI. to found a hall in Oxford for a president and fellows. This he established, under the name of St. Mary Magdalen, in certain buildings on the south side of the High Street, of which he obtained a lease from St. John's Hospital, to which the premises belonged. The hall was dissolved, and the members received into the college immediately after its foundation. William of Waynflete took his surname, according to a common custom of the clergy, from the place of his birth, a sea-port town on the coast of Lincolnshire. He had his education in Wykeham's colleges at Winchester and Oxford; was school-master of the former several years, and in 1440 was removed to Eton College by the royal founder, Henry VI. Waynflete was a constant adherent, through all his troubles, to that unfortunate prince; who always regarded him with the greatest confidence, and appointed him a trustee in his last will and testament. He was sometime provost of Eton College; and in 1447 was promoted to the bishopric of Winchester, over which he presided with consummate prudence during many years, notwithstanding the political distractions of the times. He died in 1486, and lies buried in Winchester Cathedral, within a chapel of exquisite architecture.

† Life of William of Waynflete, Bishop of Winchester, by Richard Chandler, D.D., 1811, p. 137.

divided from it by two tall columns and a pair of arches, on each side. The choir was furnished with stalls for the clergy and members of the college: and at the upper end stood the high altar, where mass was solemnly celebrated with music. Beyond this, the eastern wall of the chapel had no window, but was covered with tracery, and richly sculptured tabernacles filled with statues. In the outward part of the chapel were placed several smaller altars, for the private celebration of mass.* Such was the original state of the chapel of this college, as well as of those of New College and All Souls. The hall is joined to the east end of the chapel, and their walls and roofs are of equal breadth and elevation. Other buildings surround an outward court, in front of the chief entrance and of the west end of the chapel: there are also considerable buildings on the south side of the hall and chapel, facing the High Street, and particularly a lofty and noble tower, containing a peal of bells.

This brief sketch of the history and general description of this magnificent college has been thought necessary to a proper explanation of the parts selected as examples of its original architecture: a more ample account would be inconsistent with the plan of the present work.

PLATE I. DOORWAY AT THE WEST END OF MAGDALEN COLLEGE CHAPEL.

As the western front of the chapel of Magdalen College forms part of the principal range of buildings in the outer court, the architects were careful to adorn its entrance with a becoming richness of ornament. The subject of the three following Plates has scarcely its equal in the display of so much elegance, on a scale comparatively small. Of the five little statues on the battlements which form the most prominent ornament in the general design, that in the centre represents St. Mary Magdalen, the titular saint of the college. The next, on the dexter side, is thought to have been intended for King Henry III. in whose reign the hospital, anciently standing on the site of the college, was re-edified.† The farthest figure on the same side represents St. John the

---

* At All Souls chapel there were six altars in the aisles, and one in the vestibule, besides the high altar.

† Could we suppose that the triumphant monarch of the house of York would allow the statue of his rival to be set up after his defeat, this figure might be attributed with probability to King Henry VI., to whose patronage Bishop Waynflete was principally indebted for his promotion. The kneeling posture suits well with the devout character of that unfortunate prince. Nor is there any thing in the appearance of the figure to contradict the supposition of its being intended to represent Henry VI., who is always shewn with a shaven chin, as in this statue; whilst Henry III., on the contrary, wore his beard, as we find by the monumental statue of that sovereign.

Baptist, the patron of the hospital. On the other side of the central statue stands that of a bishop, commonly attributed to William of Wykeham: if this appropriation be correct, it was placed as a memorial of gratitude to the friend of his early years, by the pious founder,* whose figure is seen in the next niche, in a kneeling posture, the humble attitude in which he chose to be represented on the seal of his college, as well as on the entrance tower.† The panels on each side of the central niche are sculptured with the badge of King Edward IV. the reigning sovereign at the time of the building, and that of the founder; and in the spandrils of the arch are their arms, placed beneath the corresponding badges.

PLATE II. SECTIONS AND MOULDINGS AT LARGE OF THE DOORWAY.

A complete section of the door, taken perpendicularly through the centre of the arch, is here given, in order to shew the depth of the porch, with its projection, and the thickness of the wall to which it is attached; together with enlarged profiles of various mouldings belonging to the component parts of the general design.

PLATE III. VARIOUS DETAILS OF THE DOORWAY.

In the upper part of this Plate are shewn the canopy and base of one of the five niches, in the battlements over the door ; both as they appear in front, and also in sections through the centre. Next to these are half-length figures placed at the ends of the label, or hood-mould, which covers the arch. Both are intended to represent angels. The first is clothed, and holds a shield sculptured with the arms of Waynflete. The second is covered with feathers, after a fashion in which those celestial beings were commonly represented by the artists of the fifteenth century, and bears in his hands a long stalk with lilies, a flower which formed the favourite badge of the founder.‡

* St. Swithin, Bishop of Winchester, being named among the patron saints of the college, this statue might possibly be intended for him, though it has hitherto been ascribed to William of Wykeham.

† The statue of Bishop Wykeham appears in the same position on both fronts of the tower of his college at Winchester.

‡ The adoption of this flower seems to have been made by the bishop in allusion to the salutation of the blessed Virgin Mary, (St. Luke, i. 26), in which the old artists commonly represented the Angel Gabriel with a white lily in his hand, as an emblem of virginal purity; and a flower-pot with a lily springing out of it also forms an ornament in some old pictures of the same event.

Below these are shewn three of the four panels which fill up the spaces between the niches. The first is merely architectural, having an ornament of foliage placed in the centre; and the farthest panel on the opposite side, in the work itself, is of a similar pattern. The next exhibits a rose, placed upon a radiant sun; an heraldic device adopted by king Edward IV. and others of his family, in commemoration of the appearance of three suns in the sky, immediately conjoining into one, which are said to have been seen before the battle at Mortimer's Cross, near Ludlow, where Edward, then Earl of March, obtained a great victory on Candlemas-day, 1461.* The other device is formed of lilies, disposed in form of a cross. A section, and two portions of the *hood-mould*,† are shewn in the bottom part of the plate. The hollow moulding, or *casement*, is filled with the lily, repeated in a series of delicate sculpture. The same flower is also seen in the arms of Waynflete, which appear on a shield in one of the spandrils of the arch.‡ The shield is surrounded with the garter, inscribed with its appropriate motto, the bishop of Winchester bearing the office of prelate of that most noble order.

PLATE IV. The choir of Magdalen college chapel consists of five bays, or compartments, divided by slender buttresses, gradually reducing as they ascend, and finished with pinnacles. There is a general correspondence both in design and dimensions to the chapel of All Souls College, with something more of simplicity in the details,§ particularly in the windows, which have their heads turned in simple pointed arches, instead of the

---

* Shakspeare alludes to this in the soliloquy of Richard, Duke of Gloucester, spoken with reference to the triumph of his family in the exaltation of his brother Edward IV. to the crown:

"Now is the winter of our discontent
Made glorious summer by this *sun* of York;
And all the clouds that lower'd upon our house
In the deep bosom of the ocean buried!"

Richard III. Act I. Scene I.

† This moulding is improperly called a *string-course* in the engraved Plate. It is frequently termed a *label*, but *hood-mould* is the term used by the old masons. See Glossary to "Specimens of Gothic Architecture."

‡ The bishop added three lilies on a chief to his family arms, taking the augmentation from the arms of Eton College, in grateful acknowledgment of his former preferment. See "Vetusta Monum." Vol. III.

§ See Plate II. of the Chapel of All Souls College.

compound arch, with an obtuse point, which was so prevalent in the fifteenth century, and which is found in the windows of All Souls Chapel. One compartment is here given in an external elevation, together with a section through the wall and buttress, and some details of mouldings on an enlarged scale. The roof, partly shewn in the section, is modern, and very different from that originally placed on the chapel. The ancient roof was framed with open trusses of timber, carved and moulded on the inside, in a similar style to the roof of All Souls chapel, and rising to the ridge with a very low inclination; so that the outside was concealed by the embattled parapets. This roof being decayed, the architect employed to rebuild it, instead of following the taste of his predecessors, put up a plaster ceiling, in imperfect resemblance of a groined vault; while the external roof was raised to such a disproportionate height, that the openings of the battlements were half blocked up, in order to keep the roof a little more out of sight.* Such instances of overweening conceit, too proud to copy, though unable to improve, deserve to be exposed, as warnings against future offences.

PLATE V. Several details appertaining to the entrance-tower of Magdalen College have been here brought together for particular illustration.

No. 1 is a very curious example of a chimney, in which the three tunnels it contains are covered over with small arches, above which rises a pinnacle, corresponding to those at the angles of the tower. Chimneys were very rare before the reign of Henry VII. and but few perfect specimens are found of an earlier date.

No. 2 shews the upper part of the stair-turret at the south-east angle of the tower, the situation of which is seen in the annexed plan of the roof of the tower.

PLATE VI. ORIEL WINDOW NEAR THE GREAT ENTRANCE.

There is nothing particularly worthy of remark in the design of this window, which, however, possesses considerable elegance when viewed in perspective. The mouldings are boldly struck, so that their deep curves may produce a strong effect of light and shadow, a circumstance which the artists of those days always attended to, and generally with success.

* Similar alterations were made at the same time in the roof and battlements of the college hall, to the great injury of this magnificent range of buildings, as viewed externally.

PLATE VII.—VIII. The entrance-tower of Magdalen College may fairly be ranked amongst the most beautiful examples of its kind; the gracefulness of the whole composition, and the elegance of its details, being equally admirable. A plate of double size has been appropriated to this exquisite piece of architecture, for the better display of two complete elevations, on a scale sufficiently large to make their details intelligible. This tower stands in the western range of the cloistered quadrangle, with the outward front looking into the first court of the college, very near to its north side, which is formed by the lodgings of the president. These apartments were erected in 1485, and originally exhibited a front of two stories, embattled, and adorned with windows of corresponding style to those of the adjoining buildings. But, about sixty years since, this front was raised to the height of three stories, and the windows were reduced to the modern domestic fashion; mere naked perforations, devoid of mullions, or any other architectural ornament. At the time of this deplorable mutilation of so important a part of the college buildings, the passage through the grand entrance was closed; and the visitor is now conducted into the college by a narrow side door, adjoining to the chapel, and so enters the cloisters at the south-west corner, instead of proceeding into the quadrangle directly through the grand portal. The plan of the entrance is shewn on the Plate, at A, where the lateral openings into the cloisters are seen, and also the arrangement of the ribs in the vaulted roof.

The height of the tower to the battlements is rather above twice that of the adjoining buildings of the quadrangle; and the same proportion is found in the towers of several other colleges and castellated mansions, where the ranges of habitable apartments seldom exceeded two floors in height before the time of Queen Elizabeth, whilst the towers commonly had four, as we find in the example under consideration. The bay-window, which forms the most prominent feature of the front, rests its projection upon the arch of the great gateway, which has a pair of ribs with perforated spandrils, detached from the solid arch in which the doors are hung. The lower portion of the window gives light to a spacious room, which retains the name of the founder's chamber. (See the plan B.) The openings of this part of the window have been deprived of their tracery, which originally corresponded to that in the upper lights. This mutilation seems the only considerable injury that any part of the design has suffered. Of the four statues which adorn this front, that standing in the upper niche on the north side of the window represents St. Mary Magdalen, and the opposite one St. John the Baptist. Beneath the latter is the figure of Bishop Waynflete, kneeling; and opposite to him is a statue in the same attitude, royally habited and crowned, which has hitherto been ascribed to King Henry III., but which appears evidently to be a portrait of Henry VI.*

The eastern face of the tower has exactly the same arrangement of windows as the opposite one. The arch over the gateway has only a plain contour of mouldings, without the detached ribs seen in the other front;† and there are no statues on this side, excepting two small figures bearing the arms of Waynflete.

The turret on the left hand constitutes the most striking difference between this and the outward front of the tower. It contains a spiral staircase leading to the different chambers and the roof: and here it may not be impertinent to remark, how boldly the old architects transgressed that regular and uniform correspondence of parts to which their modern imitators so scrupulously confine themselves. Such irregularity has been censured as inconsistent with critical theories; but to its practice we owe a great deal of the picturesque and scenic effect which characterises the architecture of the middle ages.

On a comparison of this magnificent tower with those of the other colleges, we shall find here a more decided resemblance to the ecclesiastical style, particularly in the slender, graduated buttresses, and the crocketed pinnacles, which are peculiar to the entrance-tower of Magdalen College.

PLATE IX. On the left hand of this Plate will be found the canopy and pedestal of one of the niches which adorn the west front of the tower, with a plan of the same, shewing the tracery under the canopy. The opposite half of the Plate is filled with details of the tracery and mouldings

---

* See what has been noticed in regard of the small figure of a king over the west door of the chapel. If this appropriation be correct, the statues were probably set up after the restoration of the house of Lancaster to the sovereignty, by the accession of Henry VII., A.D. 1485. The founder survived this event exactly one year.

† This detached arch is a feature of uncommon design. We find it repeated, on a smaller scale, in the western door of the college chapel; and there is another instance in the south porch of Sefton church, in Lancashire, which was rebuilt, and most curiously adorned, by some of the family of Molineux, ancestors of the earls of Sefton; but in this instance, the spandrils of the arch are filled with carving, and not perforated as these are at Magdalen College.

in the screen which crosses the west front under the bay window; and beneath those details, one of the ornaments of the detached arch over the gateway.

PLATE X. No. 1 shews a part of the frieze which extends across the eastern front of the tower, between the principal arch and the bay window.

Nos. 2 and 3 are parts of the bay windows, with the embattled parapets on the top, and the panels beneath the upper lights. No. 4 shews a part of the vaulted roof over the gateway, both as to its plan and the curvature of the ribs.

BRAZENNOSE COLLEGE, OXFORD.

Founded 1512.

THE principal buildings of this college surround a quadrangular court, with a tower over the entrance in the eastern front. The ground on which the college stands had been occupied, previously to its foundation, by several *hostels*, or *halls*, for the lodging of students, of which the chief one was distinguished by the name of Brazennose Hall, from a masque, or large nose of brass, affixed by way of sign to the front door; and this sign has continued to designate the college down to the present time.*

The date of 1509, inscribed over a door which originally led to the chapel, probably records the commencement of the college buildings, which were prepared to receive the members in 1512, though not then finished.

Brazennose Hall is thought to have stood where is now the entrance-tower, and to have been one of the last parts of the ancient edifices to be rebuilt. The expense of covering this tower with lead, amounting to 12*l.* 1*s.* 2*d.*, was paid by three annual instalments, of which the first was discharged in 1517; and this record ascertains the time when the subject under consideration was finished.

The front of Brazennose tower bears a general resemblance to that of

---

* See "The Lives of William Smyth, bishop of Lincoln, and Sir Richard Sutton, knight, founders of Brazennose College," by the Rev. Ralph Churton, M.A. 8vo. 1800.

Magdalen College, which its architect evidently had in view, and probably intended to rival. The canted window in the third story has its model in Magdalen tower, but here it rises from a flat screen, which is terminated by an embattled parapet, the front being covered with panels of tracery, interwoven with the mullions of two windows, which give light to the principal chamber.* The substitution of this screen, instead of a continuation of the canted window in two stories, as we see in the tower of Magdalen College, rather injures the simplicity of the design, though it detracts nothing from its richness. The niches in the upper story are all vacant, and perhaps were never filled with statues. The two lower ones were probably intended for figures of St. Chad, bishop of Lichfield, and St. Hugh, bishop of Lincoln; and the smaller niche in the centre for an emblematic representation of the blessed Trinity, as they appear upon the college seal.

The royal arms of Henry VIII. are sculptured immediately over the arch of the gate; the bearings being those of France and England quarterly, supported by a dragon and a greyhound, with the crown held over the shield by two angels. This beautiful tower is not so lofty as that over the entrance of Magdalen College, but is about the same height as that of All Souls, and originally bore a similar proportion to the adjoining ranges of the front, being about twice their height, before a third story was added to them, in the reign of James I., an addition which injured the effect of the tower, by lessening its apparent elevation.

ST. PETER'S CHURCH, OXFORD.

This church has been much celebrated by the admirers of ancient architecture, as an undoubted example of the Saxon style. The Oxford antiquary, Thomas Hearne, asserted that it was built by St. Grymbald, a learned monk, whom King Alfred invited into this country, and who became

* These windows were rudely deprived of their mullions, for the insertion of two square wooden sashes, but are now restored to their proper form.

professor of divinity in the University of Oxford, on its foundation by Alfred, in the ninth century.* But these pretensions, when brought to the test of impartial criticism, have been found destitute of substantial proof. The great Alfred is no longer regarded as the founder of the university, nor had the learned Grymbald any share in its establishment. The architecture of St. Peter's Church must be placed on a lower scale of antiquity, and, like many other edifices heretofore regarded as *pure Saxon*, must take its rank among the numerous edifices erected within the first century after that grand architectural epoch, the Norman conquest.† St. Peter's Church is, however, a very interesting structure; and its vaulted chancel, with the crypt beneath it, are particularly curious. The porch which forms the subject of the two plates was probably added to the more ancient building in the reign of King Henry V. Hearne has recorded that, the church being much out of repair, a dispute arose between the parishioners and the inhabitants of Wolvercote, a chapelry dependent on St. Peter's, who refused, when called upon, to contribute a third part of the expense of repair. The litigation of this question began in 1413, and was determined in 1416;‡ soon after which time we may fairly presume to place the erection of the porch.

PLATE I. gives an elevation and section of the front of the south porch.

PLATE II. shews the plan, with an external elevation of the west side, and two sections.

The construction of the roofs to the porch and the chamber over it are particularly worthy of examination, both being formed of stone, with great neatness and ingenuity; indeed, the whole structure is very completely and

---

* See the Latin discourse, addressed by Hearne to Brown Willis, prefixed to the 1st volume of Leland's "Collectanea," with engravings. Alfred died in the year 900; his venerable counsellor and chaplain, the abbot Grymbald, in 903; and both were buried at Winchester.

† In Britton's "Architectl. Antiqs." Vol. IV., page 121, is an essay on the history of St. Peter's Church, contributed to that work by a gentleman of Oxford. See also Vol. V. of the same work, in which are two plates representing the crypt under the chancel, with a short disquisition on its age, at p. 200.

‡ Account of some Antiquities in and about Oxford, appended to the 2d Vol. of Leland's "Itinerary," p. 107. Second edition. 1745.

nicely finished.* The porch of a church was anciently used for the performance of several religious ceremonies appertaining to baptism, matrimony, and the solemn commemoration of Christ's passion in Holy Week, &c. It was also the place where the parishioners assembled for civil purposes. The chamber over it was generally used for the keeping of books and records belonging to the church. Such an appendage was added to many churches in the fourteenth and fifteenth centuries; and some of these old libraries still remain, with their books fastened to the shelves or desks by small chains.

ST. MARY'S CHURCH, OXFORD.

ST. MARY'S, or the University Church, is a fine example of the ecclesiastical architecture of the fifteenth century, and is particularly admired for the graceful elevation of its tower and spire, which, however, are of an earlier date than the church itself. The body of the church is supported by clustered columns and sharp-pointed arches; but the arches of the windows in the aisles and clerestory are obtusely pointed, shewing the gradual progress of the flattened arch, which at last superseded the more simple form almost entirely. All the windows are filled with rectilinear tracery, of similar patterns, though their sizes and forms vary. The roofs are nearly flat, and are framed of beams and rafters neatly moulded, and supported by arched spandrils, carved in tracery.†

PLATE I. shews an elevation of one bay or compartment of the nave and south aisle, taken externally; together with details of mouldings and tracery on an enlarged scale.

PLATE II. represents a compartment of the choir, with a section, and enlarged details.

---

* The porch of St. Michael's Church, Oxford, has a slight resemblance to this of St. Peter's, but is smaller, and has no chamber over it. See "Specimens of Gothic Architecture," Vol. II. Plate XIX. p. 10.

† See a Plate containing sections, &c. of this spire, in Vol. I. of "Specimens of Gothic Architecture," and the accompanying account, at p. 24. Also two Plates of sections of St. Mary's Church, in Vol. II. of the same work, with a short description, at p. 8.

PLATE III. The three stalls here represented are attached to the south side of the chancel, near to the high altar: they were intended for the priest, with his attendants, the deacon and sub-deacon, to sit in whilst certain parts of the mass were sung by the choir. Such stalls have been often described as *confessionals* by persons ill-acquainted with ecclesiastical antiquity; but their real use is well known, and admits of no doubt. These stalls in St. Mary's Church are designed with elegance and delicacy. The mouldings are remarkably simple, but sufficiently enriched by ornaments of foliage to produce a very good effect.

ST. KATHARINE'S CHURCH, TOWER HILL, LONDON.

THIS church was attached to an hospital originally founded by Matilda of Boulogne, wife of King Stephen, in the year 1148. In 1273, it was refounded by Alianora, or Eleanor, queen of Henry III., and was improved by the benefactions of Philippa, the consort of Edward III. The queens of England were always patronesses of this establishment, which escaped the destruction that overwhelmed nearly all such foundations at the change of religion, and it is still in existence. The church consisted of a nave and aisles, measuring 69 feet in length, by 60 in breadth; a choir, without aisles, 63 feet long, and 32 broad; and a small modern tower attached to the ancient west front. The choir was erected in the reign of Edward III., about the middle of the fourteenth century, and the nave and aisles not long afterwards. The original architecture of this church had been highly adorned, but had latterly become much obscured and vitiated by decay and a succession of modern reparations. The whole pile has been swept away, together with the adjoining cemetery, within the last five years, to make room for the great commercial docks, to which the name of the patroness of the hospital, St. Katharine, has been strangely applied.[*]

The subject of the accompanying Plate was taken from one of the stalls,

---

[*] The establishment has been removed into the Regent's Park, where a new chapel, with a house for the master, and two ranges of apartments for the habitation of the brethren and sisters, have been erected, from the designs of Ambrose Poynter, Esq., architect.

of which there were originally thirteen on each side of the choir. The architectural lines are struck out in bold and graceful curves, and the foliage of the crockets is remarkably neat. This is a pleasing little example of the style of that period when St. Katharine's Hospital enjoyed the patronage of queen Philippa, whose portrait, with that of her royal spouse, Edward III., was displayed amongst the sculptured ornaments of the stalls.*

ST. ALBAN'S ABBEY, HERTS.

PLATE 1. No. 1. The door here represented belongs to a chapel behind the high altar of the abbey church, where the shrine of St. Alban anciently stood. It formed part of the works of William Wallingford, who presided as abbot from 1476 to 1484; or of John Whethamstead, who died in 1464. No. 2 is taken from a small chapel on the north side of the choir, erected by abbot Thomas Ramryge, for his own sepulchre, in the reign of King Henry VIII. This is a curious example of the latest style of Gothic architecture, shewing a profusion of ornaments, but wanting the graceful design which distinguished the works of the preceding age. The panels are raised in form of folded scrolls, or drapery; a fashion which began in the reign of Henry VIII., and continued to that of Elizabeth, and was frequently applied to the wainscot panels and doors of domestic apartments.† The Latin text is taken from the canticle of Hezekiah, king of Judah, recorded by the prophet Isaiah, chap. xxxviii. ver. 10,‡ which formed part of the office of the dead in the ancient liturgy. Above it is the date of construction.§

---

* Several of these ornaments are shewn in Vol. II. of "Specimens of Ancient Sculpture and Painting," published by the late John Carter, F.S.A. In folio. 1787.

† At the upper end of the hall of Magdalen College, Oxford, is a screen filled with this sort of scrolls; the stalls of Henry VII.'s Chapel and the gates of St. James's Palace have also similar panels.

‡ Thus translated from the Vulgate version:—"𝕴 𝖘𝖆𝖎𝖉, 𝕴𝖓 𝖙𝖍𝖊 𝖒𝖎𝖉𝖘𝖙 𝖔𝖋 𝖒𝖞 𝖉𝖆𝖞𝖘 𝕴 𝖘𝖍𝖆𝖑𝖑 𝖌𝖔 𝖙𝖔 𝖙𝖍𝖊 𝖌𝖆𝖙𝖊𝖘 𝖔𝖋 𝖍𝖊𝖑𝖑."

§ Abbot Ramryge died in the year 1524, or about that time; after which the abbey was given *in commendam* to Cardinal Wolsey.

BEDDINGTON CHURCH, SURREY.

The Church of Beddington, near Croyden, in Surrey, is thought to have been erected by Sir Nicholas Carew, knight, lord of the manor, in the early part of the fifteenth century. On the south side of the chancel is a chapel, containing monuments for several persons of this family, to which it was appropriated as a place of sepulture.

PLATE I. shews one of the arches and columns which separate this chapel from the chancel, together with one of the open screens which complete the partition. The details of mouldings, both in the columns and screens, are drawn on a large scale, with notes of reference.

TOMB OF SIR RICHARD CAREW,

IN BEDDINGTON CHURCH.

SIR RICHARD CAREW, the person commemorated by this monument, was a man of great consequence in the reigns of Henry VII. and Henry VIII. He was created a knight banneret at the battle of Blackheath, A.D. 1497, held the office of sheriff of Surrey, and of Sussex, more than once; and was appointed to the important trust of lieutenant of Calais by Henry VII. This place continued in his keeping after the accession of Henry VIII. by whom a patent for it was granted to Sir Richard Carew, and Sir Nicholas, his son, for the term of their lives. Sir Richard Carew died in 1520, and lies here buried; together with his second wife, Malyne, daughter of Robert Oxenbridge, Esq. of Forden, in Sussex. Their portraits, engraved on brass plates, are affixed to the table of the tomb; and round the edge are the following imperfect remains of an inscription, also engraved on brass :—

. . . . Wyfe, whiche S^r. Richard decessyd the xxiii. day of May, anno Dñi. M. V^c XX. the said Dame Malyn dyed the . . . . . day of . . . . . An . . M.V$\mathfrak{C}$ . . . *

* This epitaph was mutilated before the end of the seventeenth century, when John Aubrey, Esq. copied it for his "History of Surrey," published, several years after his death, in 1718. The

The central shield, on the cornice, is charged with the arms of Carew, with a quartering, impaled with Oxenbridge; the bearings of Sir Richard and his lady. The two lesser shields bear their respective arms, separately. This monument gives a very fair example of the latest fashion of ornamented sepulchres, before the pointed, or Gothic, style of architecture became superseded by the Italian. The projection of the tomb is shewn in the section, and the recess of the arch, which is cut into the substance of the wall, is pointed out by the shaded lines drawn on the elevation.

BEDDINGTON MANOR HOUSE, SURREY.

THE mansion of the Carew family, at Beddington, is an extensive edifice of brick, composed of a spacious hall in the centre, with two wings of a different style, and of subsequent erection. The hall, which has a fine roof of timber, is said to have been erected by Sir Francis Carew, knt., grandson to Sir Richard, whose tomb has been described above. He died in 1611, at a very advanced age.

The lock on the principal door of the hall, represented in the accompanying Plate, No. 1, is most curiously wrought. The date of this elaborate piece of workmanship must be referred to the reign of Henry VII., whose arms are sculptured in the centre, upon a plate which slides over the keyhole, so as to conceal it.* The other enrichments shew various imitations, in miniature, of architectural decorations of that period. Examples of this sort of furniture are very rarely seen; but a few perfect specimens may occasionally be found, sufficient to prove how carefully the most subordinate

---

latter part was probably never completed; the date of her death being left for her executors to insert, by the lady herself, when she erected the monument over her husband's grave, intending it to serve also for her own sepulchre. Many similar instances of posthumous neglect may be seen on the monuments of the dead.

* These armorial bearings are appropriated to Henry VII. by the supporters, a dragon and a greyhound collared, which are placed on each side of the shield. Beneath appear two roses, the celebrated badges of the rival families of Lancaster and York, united by the marriage of this king.

appendages of ancient architecture were finished in accordance with the proper style.

No. 2.—This is an ancient handle for a door, of which the ring is attached to a circular plate, richly worked in an architectural pattern, of the same style as the lock at Beddington Hall.*

No. 3. Shews a small lock for a chest, of the same date as the larger example. It is prettily ornamented with patterns of foliage.

ARCHIEPISCOPAL PALACE, AT CROYDON, SURREY.

THE manor of Croydon was given by King William the Conqueror to Lanfranc, the celebrated Archbishop of Canterbury, who filled the metropolitical see from 1070 to 1089. There was certainly a mansion here, with a chapel attached to it, in the thirteenth century, and it had probably been an occasional residence for the archbishops at a much earlier period. From some passages in the registers, it has been inferred that the buildings were at first constructed entirely with timber, and that the mansion was only of very narrow dimensions; but the expressions on which these opinions were grounded, seem to have been misunderstood. The present buildings appear to have been erected in the fifteenth century, by the Archbishops Arundel, Stafford, and their successors. Matthew Parker, the first Protestant archbishop, entertained Queen Elizabeth at Croydon Palace during a whole week, in July, 1575. After the execution of Archbishop Laud, and the abolition of the episcopal dignity, this palace was seized by authority of the parliament, and let out on lease to lay tenants; but it was recovered at the restoration of King Charles II. in 1660, and continued to be inhabited, at different times, by several archbishops, down to the year 1757, when Dr. Thomas Herring, the last prelate who resided here, died and was buried at Croydon. The palace

---

* When the fret-work was pierced through the plate, a piece of crimson velvet or cloth was sometimes put under it, so as to be seen in the openings. The handles on the doors of some chapels in Lincoln Minster were lined in this manner.

was deserted after this period; and, in 1780, an act of parliament was passed to enable Archbishop Cornwallis to alienate the buildings with some adjoining land, in order to erect a new palace on a more elevated and dry situation, as a summer residence for himself and his successors.* The premises were then sold, and the palace became degraded to the uses of a manufactory, by which its venerable buildings have been sadly injured and disfigured. The whole pile nearly resembled a college, being composed of various buildings, some constructed of stone and some of brick, arranged round a quadrangular court, of an oblong, irregular plan, about 52 yards wide from east to west, and 72 from north to south. The principal gate was on the north side, opposite to the hall, which occupied the centre of the southern range of buildings, in which were the chief apartments. The palace appears to have been anciently surrounded by a moat, the situation being well suited to that mode of fortification, which was seldom neglected where a supply of water could be had.

PLATE I.—THE HALL OF CROYDON PALACE.

The form of this apartment will be best explained by reference to the ground-plan, which is given entire, though on a small scale, shewing the plan of the roof, as well as of the walls, windows, porch, &c. The section represents the east end of the hall, together with one of the timber arches supporting the roof, which is framed in four bays. The porch, which projects from the north side towards the court, has a vaulted roof, over which was formerly a chamber, with a chimney in one corner. This was the principal entrance, and opposite to it is another, opening into the gardens. The three arched doors in the eastern wall led to the buttery, kitchen, and cellar; and above them was originally a lofty window, overlooking the music-gallery, which has been entirely removed, together with the screen that supported it. In the place of the great window, a very curious piece of sculpture has been inserted, which appears to have been removed from another part of the palace, when the hall was fitted up by Archbishop Herring. The royal arms of France and England, quarterly, are impaled with those ascribed to King Edward the Confessor. The shield is supported by two angels, and surmounted by an arched or imperial crown. At the bottom is another angel, bearing a scroll inscribed

* The intention of erecting a new palace was not carried into effect; but by a subsequent act of parliament, passed in 1807, a mansion was purchased at Addington, near Croydon, which has since been enlarged and improved, and is now the country seat of the archbishops of Canterbury.

with this motto, **Domine salvum fac regem,** "Lord save the king!" A square tester, or canopy, projects over the whole sculpture, which is very highly wrought in bold relief. This piece of ornament is probably of the same date as the hall itself, as may be inferred from the mouldings attached to the lower part, which correspond exactly to those in the cornice surrounding the hall. The arms have been attributed to King Henry VI., and are supposed to have been put up by Archbishop John Stafford, who sat from 1443 to 1452. The erection of the hall may be ascribed to this prelate with great probability, as his arms are emblazoned upon some of the shields on the cornice, both singly, impaled with those of the see of Canterbury, and also impaled with those of the bishoprick of Bath and Wells, which he held before his promotion to the primacy. On other shields are the arms of Humphrey, Earl of Stafford, created Duke of Buckingham in 1444; of Henry, his son and successor in his titles; and of Richard Plantagenet, Duke of York, who fell in the battle of Wakefield, A.D. 1460; to which have been added those of the Archbishops Laud, Juxon, and Herring. These shields were probably new coloured at the time the hall was repaired by the prelate last mentioned, when the louvre on the roof, over the hearth in the middle of the hall, was destroyed, and other alterations were made.

PLATE II.—No. 1. shews a vertical section of one bay, or compartment, taken in the centre of the roof.

No. 2. gives an exterior elevation of the same portion of the south side, including the door opening towards the garden.

No. 3. A longitudinal section of the whole building is here given on a small scale, shewing the interior elevation of the south side. The oriel, or bay-window, which occupies the western compartment, has only a low arch, placed beneath the cornice and upper windows, instead of being carried up to the whole height of the wall, as was generally done.

No. 4. Parts of a window are here exhibited on an enlarged scale.

In the centre of the plate, above the exterior elevation, will be found a section of the mouldings in one of the principal arches of the roof, taken at their junction in the centre.

In concluding this description, it may be observed, that the hall of Croydon Palace, though not an example of the first class, was a noble room, finished in a neat and pleasing style of architecture; and the admirer of antiquity will regret that its preservation was not secured by appropriation to some decent purpose, at the time when the palace was abandoned by its reverend possessors, after almost seven centuries of occupation.

PLATE III.—The subject of this plate is taken from an apartment called the Guard-room. It was one of the chief apartments in the palace, after the hall and chapel. It is said to have been erected by Archbishop Arundel, in the beginning of the fifteenth century, his arms being found on two corbels within the chamber; but the bay-window here represented is certainly of a later date, by nearly a century, if not more. This window is neatly formed, but has nothing uncommon about it, nor does it require any verbal description.

CHAPEL OF CROYDON PALACE.

THERE were formerly two chapels attached to the Archiepiscopal Palace, of which the larger, or principal chapel, as it is called in the registers, served for the use of the household; and several ordinations of clergymen were also held in it: the smaller chapel served for the archbishop's private devotions; but this has entirely perished. The present chapel is an oblong building of brick, finished with remarkable plainness. No part of its architecture appears older than the middle of the sixteenth century, though it is free from any admixture of the Italian style; and from the frugality of its construction, so unsuitable to the ancient magnificence of the metropolitan prelates, it seems most probable that the chapel was rebuilt after the impoverishment of the see of Canterbury in the reign of Edward VI. The papal badge of the cross-keys, twice repeated in brick-work on the western gable, certainly could not have been set up by Archbishop Parker, nor any of his Protestant successors: perhaps the chapel was rebuilt by Cardinal Pole, who held the Archbishoprick of Canterbury during the reign of Queen Mary. It received some embellishment from the unfortunate Archbishop Laud; but was desecrated in the time of the Commonwealth, and again repaired and consecrated by Dr. Juxon, after the restoration of the hierarchy, in 1660. Since the sale of the palace, and its conversion into a manufactory, the chapel has been used as a schoolhouse, and consequently has been better preserved than the hall and other buildings.* A small turret, containing a bell, which formerly stood upon the west end of the roof, has been taken down; the other parts remain entire.

PLATE I.—No. 1. gives a transverse section of the chapel, taken in two different parts; half of the screen, which divides the choir from the ante-chapel, being shewn on the right hand of the central line, the other half shewing a portion of the choir and of the eastern window.

No. 2. The general plan of the chapel is here given on a small scale. The irregularity of the west end was occasioned by the oblique position of the palace buildings towards the churchyard, from which there is an approach to the chapel by a porch and a flight of stairs at the north-west angle, opposite to another door leading into the palace.

No. 3. shews part of the ceiling, which is constructed of wood, and is divided into square panels, by moulded ribs. From the arrangement of the timbers, the roof appears to have been originally finished in a low pitch, with gutters and parapets at the side, and afterwards raised by the addition of rafters adapted to a covering of tiles, instead of lead.

PLATE II.—No. 1. A compartment of the north side is here shewn, in a section taken along the central line of the roof.

No. 2. gives details of the mouldings on the screen, of which the upper panels are open, the lower ones close. In this screen, as well as the fronts of the desks, there is no ornamental tracery; which was generally laid aside after the reign of Henry VIII.

No. 3. This small section exhibits the whole length of the chapel, with the southern windows, the seats, gallery, &c.

* To our description of the hall must be added a mortifying piece of intelligence; viz. that the eastern gable entirely fell to the ground on the 8th of June, 1830, together with the fine sculpture of the royal arms already described; but which, fortunately, escaped uninjured by the fall.

It is given in "Pugin's Gothic Ornaments," now publishing, from a drawing taken at large on the spot.

ELTHAM PALACE, KENT.

THE agreeable situation of Eltham seems to have made it a place of some note at an early period, for the manor was a royal one in the reign of Edward the Confessor. It was given by William the Conqueror to his half-brother, Odo, Bishop of Bayeux, whom he created Earl of Kent, bestowing upon him a vast number of manors in this and other counties. On the forfeiture and banishment of this powerful prelate, for a conspiracy against William Rufus, Eltham reverted to the crown, and a moiety of it was afterwards obtained by the baronial family of Mandeville. The earliest account of a royal residence at Eltham is given by the continuator of Matthew Paris the historian, who relates that Henry III. with his queen, and the principal persons of the realm, solemnised the feast of Christmas here in 1270. Edward I. granted one half of the manor, in 1280, to John de Vesci, who married Isabella de Beaumont, a lady related to the queen. This Lord Vesci procured the moiety of Eltham which Walter de Mandeville possessed, by an exchange of other lands; and obtained a royal charter for a market to be held every Tuesday in his town of Eltham, and an annual fair of three days. John de Vesci dying without issue, in 1289, was succeeded by his brother William, who having no lawful issue to survive him, conveyed his manor of Eltham, with the honour and castle of Alnwick in Northumberland, and other estates, in 1296, to Anthony Beke, Bishop of Durham and titular Patriarch of Jerusalem, in trust for his illegitimate son John. The bishop stands accused of having violated his trust, as the young man never obtained possession of these estates. But perhaps there might be some circumstances in the business sufficient to justify his conduct, which have not come to the knowledge of posterity; for, though this prelate displayed a degree of pomp and grandeur in his establishments more becoming a temporal prince than a Christian bishop, he does not seem to have borne a bad character, and the purity of his morals is expressly attested by an ancient historian of good credit; nor could he have been guilty of any public acts of injustice without the connivance of his sovereign. However, it is certain that, in 1309, the bishop sold Alnwick castle to Henry de Percy,* and Eltham

---

* See Dugdale's Baronetage, vol. i. It was only the mansion or palace of Eltham, with some demesnes attached to it, which Bishop Beke left to the queen; for on the death of John de Vesci,

he retained in his own occupation. Anthony de Beke partook of the taste of the age in which he flourished, and raised several stately buildings. He rebuilt the manor house of Eltham, making it one of the many mansions where he occasionally resided; and at his death, which happened here in 1311, he bequeathed it to the queen Isabella, wife to Edward II. From this period Eltham began to be a regular place of royal residence; and here, in 1315, was born John of Eltham, the second son of Edward II. afterwards created Earl of Cornwall.* Edward III. held a parliament here in 1329. A.D. 1347, the king being engaged in the invasion of France, his third son, Lionel of Antwerp, Duke of Clarence, being appointed regent of England in his father's absence, kept the solemn feast of Christmas at this palace. And here, in 1364, Edward III. entertained John, King of France, who was then a prisoner of war, with magnificent feasting. Another parliament was assembled at Eltham in 1375. The royal feasts at Christmas were celebrated here in 1384, 1385, and 1386; and in the latter year Eltham was the scene of a splendid feast, when Richard II. received Leo, King of Armenia, who come to implore assistance from the Christian princes against his enemies the Turks.

That delightful historian of chivalry, Sir John Froissart, has related, with his peculiar liveliness and simplicity, how he came to Eltham in the year 1395, while Richard II. was holding a parliament, or rather a council of state, in this palace; and how he presented a volume of his Chronicles to the king, who received him in the royal bed-chamber in the most gracious manner.

Henry IV. resided frequently at Eltham, and celebrated Christmas here in the years 1405, 1409, and 1412; and in 1414, the succeeding monarch, Henry V. kept that feast at Eltham, at which time an alarm was given by sudden news of a tumultuous assembly of the Lollards in St. Giles's Fields. The feast of Christmas was again celebrated here in 1429 by Henry VI. with great magnificence.

A.D. 1480, Bridget, the third daughter of Edward IV., was born at Eltham and christened in the chapel.

The solemnities of Christmas were kept here by Edward IV. and his court in 1483, when two thousand persons were daily fed at the royal tables.

the younger, who fell in the battle of Bannockburn, in 1314, the manor of Eltham came to his kinsman and heir, Sir Gilbert de Aton, by whom it was sold soon afterwards to Geoffrey Scrope of Masham, the conveyance being confirmed by royal patent.

* See his tomb in "Specimens of Gothic Architecture," vol. ii. p. 18, Pl. XXXI.

This prince expended great sums in improving the parks and buildings at Eltham; and his badges, still remaining amongst the ornaments of the hall, bear sufficient evidence that this noble piece of architecture was part of what he erected.

Henry VII. rebuilt one front of this palace.

Henry VIII. kept the solemn feast of Christmas at Eltham in 1515, when one of those theatrical spectacles called a masque was exhibited in the great hall.

The same monarch was here again in 1526, but Christmas was not celebrated that year with the accustomed solemnities for fear of the plague, and hence was afterwards remembered by the name of *the still Christmas*. In this reign Eltham began to decline in the royal favour. New palaces were raised at Greenwich, New-Hall, or Beaulieu, in Essex, and Nonsuch, in Surrey. The stagnant waters of the moats were thought to make Eltham unwholesome, and the palace never recovered its ancient preference; though it was occasionally visited by the court so late as the year 1612, when James I. came here several times to enjoy his favourite exercise of hunting deer in Eltham parks. Upon the breaking out of the civil war in the reign of Charles I., the parliamentary general, Robert, Earl of Essex, took up his residence in this royal mansion, and here he died in 1646. It was confiscated, together with other possessions of the crown, on the death of the king; and in 1649, a survey of the palace, with all its appurtenances, was made by commissioners from the parliament, for the purpose of exposing the whole to sale as national property. In this parliamentary survey, "the capital mansion called Eltham" is said to contain one fair chapel, one great hall, forty-six rooms and offices on the ground floor, with two large cellars; and on the upper floor, seventeen lodging-rooms on the king's side, twelve on the queen's side, and nine on the prince's side, in all thirty-eight; and thirty-five bayes of building, in which were seventy-eight rooms in the offices round the court-yard, which contained one acre of ground. All the rooms were unfurnished, except the hall and chapel; and the whole building was in bad repair, and untenantable. There were three parks attached to the palace, named the Great Park, the Middle or Little Park, and Horne Park, containing altogether 1265 acres. The deer were all destroyed by the soldiers and lawless people; and a great quantity of fine oak timber was so totally cut down and wasted, that at the restoration of Charles II., scarcely a tree was left growing. The buildings were then dismantled, and have been gradually sinking under the effects of time and neglect ever since that disastrous period.*

The plan of this capacious mansion formed a quadrangular figure, of rather irregular dimensions; the west side measuring about 381 feet, including some projections at the angles; the east side 374 feet; and the north and south sides nearly 350 feet.† The whole of this area was raised about 15 feet, and surrounded by a moat of great breadth, the water flowing up to the external walls of the palace. There were two bridges over the moat, one on the north side, where was the approach to the principal gate; the other on the opposite quarter, leading towards the gardens and pleasure-grounds. Only the north bridge is now standing; the waters of the moat have been drained, and the whole of the ancient buildings swept away, with the exception of the great hall, and a building of two stories near the east end of the hall, probably a fragment of the lodgings erected by Henry VII. The great quadrangle covered nearly three acres of ground, and appears to have been divided into two courts, by the hall and other buildings which formed the middle range. The outer court, towards the north, in which were situated the offices enumerated in the survey of 1649, contained about one acre within the buildings.‡ The southern, or inner court, containing the chief lodgings, was considerably smaller; but the distribution of the plan

* A north-east view of Eltham Palace was published in 1735, by Samuel and Nathaniel Buck, in which the hall, with its embattled parapet and bay-window, appears entire; the lower part of the north gate-house is also shewn, as well as some adjoining buildings, which have since been demolished. Probably the ruined palace had not then been degraded into the offices of a farm, as no marks of such an appropriation appear in the print, and those industrious artists were very careful to give a faithful portrait of what they professed to represent; a merit which many of their successors, in these days of *picturesque effect*, are too apt to despise.

† Somerton Castle, in Lincolnshire, built also by Anthony Beke, was of a quadrangular plan, with four polygonal towers at the corners, and was encompassed by very strong banks and deep moats, beyond the walls. Robert de Graystanes, an ancient historian of the church of Durham, in his account of Bishop Beke's works, says,—"Castrum de Somerton juxta Lincoln, et manerium de Eltham juxta London, curiosissimè ædificavit; sed primum regi et secundum reginæ postea contulit."—*Anglia Sacra*, i. 754.

‡ The author of "An Historical and Descriptive Account of Eltham Palace," 8vo., 1828, has conjectured that the area was divided into "four quadrangles, two on the west side, and as many, of very inferior dimensions, on the east side," p. 42. See also page 66 of the same work. Such a division would have been inconsistent with the statement in the parliamentary survey, that the court of offices contained an acre of ground; which statement agrees very well with the actual dimensions, on the supposition of there being only one court on the north side of the hall.

cannot be clearly made out, nor the situation of the chapel, and other chief apartments, be ascertained with any accuracy.* The front erected by King Henry VII. has been described by some writers to have faced towards the north; others, with more probability, have judged it to have stood on the west side, overlooking the country towards London. The outward walls retain several projections, which originally supported large chimneys, turrets, or bay-windows, of which nothing but the basements are left. These ruins appear to have belonged to buildings of different ages, some constructed of brick, and some of stone, beneath which were spacious vaults and passages, most of them, undoubtedly, contrived for sewers, though they have been transformed by romantic imagination into passages for secret approach or retreat.

In describing the architecture of this beautiful hall, it may perhaps be best to commence with a reference to the plan inserted in the double plate (numbered IV. and V. in the series). The internal dimensions are 101 feet 4 inches by 36 feet; so that the length is rather less than three times the breadth, and is divided into six compartments, or *bays*, by the arched trusses which form the main supports of the roof.

Five bays are lighted by as many pairs of windows on each side; the sixth having two large oriels, or projecting windows. All the light was derived from these windows on the sides, the hall being joined at both ends to other apartments now destroyed.† The principal entrance is on the north side, close to the east end of the hall, opening from the outer court; opposite to this is another door, which led into the inner court; and a

---

* In Hasted's History of Kent, vol. i., is a plan of Eltham Palace, engraved from a drawing dated A.D. 1509, in which three ranges of apartments are shewn, enclosing a quadrangular area on the east, north, and west sides, together with some detached buildings beyond the boundaries; but, by some unaccountable error, the great hall and the chapel are not represented. The omission of these two principal apartments destroys the utility of this plan, which would have greatly assisted our description of the palace had it been tolerably exact.

† The late Edw. King, Esq., who examined this hall about fifty years ago, when it was in a more perfect state than it now is, noticed the appearance of a small window in the west gable, which he imagined to have been made for the purpose of looking into the hall from one of the chambers. It is certain that such contrivances were common in ancient halls, of which Mr. King adduced several instances; but from the great height at which this supposed window at Eltham would have been placed, and there being no appearance of it on the outside of the gable, the learned antiquary seems to have been mistaken, as he unluckily was in many other ingenious conjectures.—See *Archaeologia*, vol. vi.

communication with the kitchens, butteries, and other culinary offices, was made by two doors at the east end of the hall. All these doors were included in a passage 10 feet 6 inches wide, formed by a wooden screen crossing the lower end of the hall. Of this screen only the naked frame is now standing, stripped entirely of its ornaments. It measures about 12½ feet high, and is divided into five compartments, three of which were filled by panels and tracery, the two intermediate spaces being left open to give entrance into the hall. So far this screen resembled that in the hall of Hampton Court; and it has been generally supposed to have had a similar gallery above it, for the trumpeters and other musicians who played during high festivals, but nothing of this remains; and as there is no appearance of an approach to it, without a staircase in the hall itself, the existence of such a gallery has been doubted.*

At the upper end of the hall was a platform, raised three or four steps above the common pavement, where the high table stood, at which the principal persons sat, whilst those of inferior degrees were placed at long tables ranged down the sides of the hall. In the middle of the floor was an open hearth, and over it, in the third bay of the roof from the west end, was a louvre, or lantern, for letting out the fumes of a charcoal fire. The lantern has been taken down long since, but some rafters belonging to it are yet remaining in the roof, and from these it appears to have been of an hexagonal shape.†

On a comparison of Eltham hall with other ancient rooms of the like description, we shall find but few superior to it in dimensions, and none of finer proportions, or more scientific construction.‡

---

* The screen at Hampton Court is described in "Specimens," vol. ii. p. 6. See also an Account of Eltham Palace, by Mr. J. C. Buckler, 8vo., 1828, p. 88.

† The hall of Richmond Palace was warmed in this manner, as we find by the following description of it, made by the commissioners of parliament, A.D. 1649. "This Room hath a Screen in the lower End thereof; over which is a little Gallery, and a fayr Foot-Pace in the higher End thereof; the Pavement is square Tile, and it is very well lighted and seeled, and adorned with Eleven Statues in the Sides thereof; in the Midst a Brick Hearth for a Charcoal Fire, having a large Lanthorn in the Roof of the Hall fitted for that Purpose, turreted and covered with Lead. *Mem.*—In the North End of the great Hall there is one Turret, or Clock-Case, covered with Lead, which, together with the Lanthorn in the Middle thereof, are a special ornament unto that Building."—*Vetusta Monumenta*, vol. ii.

‡ St. George's Hall, in Windsor Castle, built by Edward III., and finished A.D. 1369, was 108 feet long by 35 broad. It had an arched roof of timber before it was modernized by Charles II.

The interior view, as it appeared when perfect, and furnished for the reception of its royal masters, must have been highly magnificent and beautiful, as we may fairly judge from the naked remains of its architecture.*

In its present condition, nothing can look more dreary:—with its windows stopped up, its sculptured ornaments mutilated, the roof broken and obscured by dust and cobwebs, and the whole fabric dilapidated, dirty, and disfigured, it forcibly reminds the spectator of the transitory nature of all human grandeur.

PLATE I.—GROINING OF THE BAY-WINDOW ON THE NORTH SIDE OF THE HALL.

A plan, or horizontal section, is here given of the upper part of one of the bay-windows, shewing the form of its vaulted roof. The key-stones to the ribs, amounting to no fewer than forty in number, are all richly sculptured with ornamental foliage, or the armorial badges of King Edward IV.; amongst which the falcon within a fetter-lock, and the *rose en soleil*, are conspicuous.

The vertical section shews the curvature of the ribs, the thickness of the vaulting taken along the central line, and the joints of the stones which compose it.

The hall of Christ-Church, Oxford, built by Cardinal Wolsey, measures 115 feet by 40.

That of Hampton Court, built by Henry VIII., is 106 feet long and 40 broad.

At New Hall, near Boreham, in Essex, another palace of Henry VIII., the hall measures 90 feet by 40, and above 40 in height.

The hall of the royal palace at Richmond was 100 feet by 40.

At Trinity College, Cambridge, the hall is 100 feet by 40. It was built in the middle of the sixteenth century.

The Middle Temple, London, has a hall built in the reign of Elizabeth, 100 feet by 44.

The hall of Lambeth Palace, rebuilt by Archbishop Juxon, in 1663, was 93 feet by 38. It has lately been converted into a library.

The Guild-Hall of the city of London, built about the year 1410, is 153 feet long and 48 wide.

The internal dimensions of Westminster Hall, rebuilt by Richard II., in 1399, are 238 feet 8 inches by 66 feet 6 inches; taking its breadth in the middle, as the south end is wider than the north. Its area is fully equal to any four of those above-mentioned, with the exception of Guildhall.

* An idea of its ancient splendour is represented in a lithographic plate of the interior of Eltham hall, in Pugin's "Series of Views illustrative of the Examples of Gothic Architecture," published in Two Parts, 4to.

PLATE II.—GROINING OF THE BAY-WINDOW ON THE NORTH SIDE OF THE HALL.

The section in the upper part of this Plate cuts across the window, shewing its projection, and the manner in which it joins to the side of the hall. The vaulted roof is cut in two places, for the purpose of more fully explaining its construction, which is extremely elaborate. The letters b b refer to the plan on the preceding Plate.

Below the transverse section is a longitudinal one, corresponding to that in the first Plate, when viewed in an opposite direction. Here is shewn the inner side of the arch opening towards the hall, as viewed within the recess of the window; and above it we see the lines of a blank arch, intended to bear the weight of the wall and roof from crushing the slender ribs of the moulded arch.

At the bottom of the Plate is given an elevation of the arch and head of the window, as seen within the hall. The tracery in the lights of these windows has a peculiarity in the curvature of the cusps, which are finished with uncommon elegance.*

PLATE III.—WINDOWS OF THE HALL, BRACKET, AND DETAILS.

No. 1. Three of the windows are here shown, in an internal elevation, with one of the stone brackets, or corbels, upon which the spandrils of the roof are placed. There are ten of these windows on each side, as was before stated, and they are set two and two together, according to the distances measured on the Plate. The general forms and proportions of these windows closely resemble those of Crosby Hall, but they are considerably larger. The mouldings are also similar; but the windows of Crosby Hall are more elaborately finished on the inside, having small columns in the jambs, and additional mouldings and tracery in the arches and spandrils.†

No. 2. Elevations of the upper and lower parts of a window are here given on an enlarged scale, with a plan of the jambs, mullion, &c.

No. 3. The front elevation, and sections of one of the stone corbels,

---

* A similar pattern is seen at Crosby Hall, London, in the ornaments of the roof of the council chamber.—See "Specimens," vol. i, Pl. XLII. It is also found in some of the tracery on the tomb of Sir Richard Carew, in Beddington Church.—See the plate in this volume.

† See "Specimens," vol. i. p. 30, Pl. XLII.*

are here given, together with part of the timber rib springing from it. These corbels resemble those in Crosby Hall, but have less of ornamental detail.

PLATE IV. and V.—THE PLAN of the hall has been already described. TRANSVERSE SECTION. This section is taken in two divisions, noted on the plan A, B, A, B. That on the right hand cuts through the centre of the timbers, and of one of the buttresses which strengthen the side walls at the feet of the trusses; it also shews an elevation of the northern bay-window on the east side.

The other division of the section cuts through the centre of the southern bay-window, and also exhibits one half of a truss with all its mouldings; and beneath this is a plan, shewing the purlines, braces, and common rafters. In the section of the bay-window is seen the door in the west side, which formerly led to other apartments westward of the hall, now destroyed. Above this door the space is covered with blank tracery, corresponding to the lights in the other sides. There is a door in the north bay, corresponding to this, adjoining to which appears to have been a narrow staircase, lighted by a small window remaining in the front of the bay, but not seen within the hall.

On comparing the roof of Eltham Hall with that of Westminster Hall, we shall find a general correspondence of parts, allowing for the superiority of scale in the latter. In the roof of Westminster Hall, the length of the rafters is a little more than four-fifths of the span, measuring across the breadth from foot to foot. In that of Eltham Hall the rafters measure something less than four-fifths of the span; consequently it is rather lower in the pitch than that of Westminster Hall. In this roof the arches are of the *compound* form, struck from four centres, with an obtuse point, after the usual forms of arches in the masonry of that age; whilst at Westminster Hall the curved timbers describe high-pointed arches, of the *simple* form, struck from two centres on the base line. The spandrils are much shorter than those at Westminster, and pendents are here introduced instead of the figures of angels. The trusses at Eltham contain a larger quantity of timber, in proportion to their breadth, than those of Westminster Hall, which the builder probably judged necessary on account of the greater lightness of the walls and buttresses at Eltham.

The gutter along the south side of the roof had formerly a parapet with a straight coping, and the cornice consists of plain mouldings. On the north side there was an embattled parapet, which has been destroyed; but the cornice remains, and is studded with grotesque heads. The two bay-windows are covered by common roofs, which are evidently modern substitutes for the original finishing. The stone cornices remain, and have sculptured heads in the centre and at the angles. The ancient roofs were probably flat, covered with lead, and surrounded by stone parapets.

The longitudinal section exhibits one compartment of the roof, cut through the ridge, together with the inside of the southern bay-window, and a part of that beyond the next corbel. The beauty of the bay-windows makes them worthy of the most careful examination.* The lights in these windows are of a tall proportion, particularly in the lower division; the bottom of those above the transom ranging in a line with the sills of the smaller windows. These were placed high above the floor, as was done in almost all ancient halls; the plain walls below the windows being generally covered with hangings of tapestry before the reign of Henry VIII., when wainscot panels were introduced, and afterwards came into common use.

In this section the purlines, braces, and cornice of one bay of the roof, are displayed, together with the profiles of two trusses. The moulding running between the cornice and the lower purline probably formed the top of a frieze, composed of ornamental tracery, which covered the feet of the rafters, such as we find in the roof of Crosby Hall, and that of Christ Church, Oxford; but not a fragment of anything of the kind now remains in Eltham Hall, excepting this plain moulding.

PLATE VI.—DOORWAY ON THE NORTH SIDE OF ELTHAM HALL.

No. 1. is an exterior elevation of the whole design, of which the details are finished in a neat and elegant style, this being the chief entrance; whilst the opposite one is of a very plain character. The arch is described from four centres, but is so little flattened at the point, that it rises very nearly one-half of the span. The blank arch over the mouldings was contrived for discharging the superincumbent weight of the wall.

No. 2. In the spandrils of this door, one of which is here given on an enlarged scale, the favourite badge of King Edward IV., a radiant sun, surmounted by a rose, is sculptured in the middle of the tracery. The date

* The southern bay-window, here represented as perfect, has been most shamefully mutilated, by cutting out all the lower part, and inserting a rude wooden frame and doors, for the passage of carts and waggons.

of the building has been determined by these badges; for before they had been observed, it was generally ascribed to an earlier period.

No. 3. These three enlarged sections of the mouldings correspond to the letters A, B, and C, marked on the elevation.

No. 4. The base and capital of one of the small columns in the jambs are here given at large, with the dimensions of their parts in figures.

This door-case nearly corresponds in general style with one in the episcopal palace at Lincoln, on which are the arms of Bishop Wm. Alnwick, who died A.D. 1449. [See "Specimens," vol. i. p. 8, Pl. XXXIX.] It has also been compared with a door on the north side of the hall at Hampton Court, leading to the *Great Chamber;* but there the arch is more flattened at the top than in this at Eltham. [See "Specimens," vol. ii. p. 7, Pl. XI.]

PLATE VII.—PENDENT, &C. IN THE ROOF OF ELTHAM HALL.

In this Plate some details of parts have been displayed on a large scale, in order to complete the explanation of the roof. The section comprehends the lower part of a truss, from the stone corbel on which it rests at the bottom to the cross-beam above the arch. The pendent is also shewn as it appears in front; together with sections of the different pieces that compose the truss, and a plan shewing the mouldings underneath. The beauty of these pendents has been much injured by their being stripped of the small pinnacles and perforated tracery with which the central pieces were originally encased. All the pendents have now lost these ornaments; but one retained them not many years since, and their form is here delineated in faint lines, to shew how they appeared when perfect.* In concluding the description of this sumptuous example of ancient carpentry, it is gratifying to mention, that it has lately been repaired at the expense of government, and thereby saved from the destruction with which it was threatened.† Yet we cannot help lamenting

* It is shewn in an interior view of Eltham Hall, in vol. i. of "Select Views of London and its Environs," published by Messrs. Storer and Greig, in 4to., 1804. See also Mr. Buckler's curious little volume, pp. 32, 78. The pendents in the roof of Christ's Church hall, Oxford, are finished in a similar style, and have been perfectly preserved.

† A question has been raised as to the quality of the timber in this roof; some persons who examined it during the repairs having stated that it was oak, while others affirm it to be of chestnut. There is great difficulty in distinguishing these pieces of timber after they have been long in use; especially where oak imported from the continent has been employed, as such timber has generally a finer grain than our English oak, which is distinguished by its superior strength and toughness. Contradictory statements have also

that these repairs were not extended to the masonry, and that the remains of Eltham Palace should not be rescued from their present degrading use, the hall cleaned and set free from the vile sheds and hovels that now disfigure its walls, and the whole site preserved from further dilapidation, and the discordant encumbrances of modern buildings.

CARVED DESK AND BENCH
IN THE CHURCH OF OLD WALSINGHAM, NORFOLK.

PLATE I.—The fastidious habits of modern times have sadly disfigured the interior appearance of our churches, by the introduction of close pews. Instead of being shut up in *square boxes*, the congregation, formerly, were seated on long benches, ranged on each side the nave of the church, with their faces turned towards the altar. This sort of furniture was perfectly suitable to the architecture of a church; the ornaments partook of the same style as the fabric itself—there was no unsightly bulk to block up the columns, which shewed their moulded bases quite down to the floor, instead of being half-buried, as they now are in most churches, amidst a heap of shapeless pews. A separate pew was a distinction appertaining only to the lord of the manor, or some other person of distinction; and it was very rarely that more than two pews were erected in the same church, before the reign of Queen Elizabeth. But these manorial pews were like small chapels, generally occupying the upper end of a north or south aile. They were enclosed by screens, enriched with perforated tracery, and were sometimes covered with canopies, and made highly ornamental. The Plate exhibits two examples of such desks and benches as the better class of parochial churches used to be furnished with. No. 1. forms the end of a desk without a seat, and is carved in the style of ornament which prevailed in the reign of Henry VIII. No. 2. is of an older fashion, and serves as the support of

been made about the use of iron in its construction. The truth is, that the roof was framed with mortices and tenons, fastened together by wooden pins, without any bolts or straps of iron; but nails were used in fixing the mouldings attached to the main timbers.

a seat, or bench. This has a low back to lean against; and behind it a narrow portion of the plank which forms the seat projects beyond the back, serving for those who sat in the range behind this to rest their arms upon, whilst they were kneeling. The sections and details of parts need no description.

In these remnants of ancient ecclesiastical furniture, we may observe a degree of skill and taste similar to what was more amply displayed in architecture; and they are deserving of being admired, both for their beauty and durability. Stout planks of oak were used for their materials, and these were carefully framed together with mortices and tenons, and fastened by pins of the same material. This solid mode of construction had a double advantage; it admitted the enrichments of moulding and carving to be worked in bold relief; and the work would endure firm and undecayed after centuries of use. The artists of those times had not learned the modern maxim, "Strength of work is the decay of trade."

OAK CEILING

IN NEW WALSINGHAM CHURCH, NORFOLK.

PLATE I.—The subject of this Plate has been selected as an example of the ornamented ceilings of the fifteenth century. Such ceilings are common to churches and the mansion-houses of the rich. Sometimes the panels were laid quite flat, and sometimes were raised from the sides, with a slight inclination towards the centre. The mouldings and ornaments admitted of endless variety, and the most elaborate and delicate carvings were frequently bestowed upon them. Such costly ceilings were generally worked in oak before the time of Henry VIII., when the use of plaster, as a cheaper material, became common. The example here displayed might serve very well as a pattern for the ceiling of a highly ornamented room, in the architectural style of Henry the VIIth's reign, and might be worked in either wood or plaster; but fine-grained oak, with the ornaments well carved, has an air of reality about it which can never be imparted to plaster, however skilfully painted.

FAKENHAM CHURCH, NORFOLK.

NORFOLK, and the adjoining county of Suffolk, contain some noble parish churches, erected, for the most part, in the fifteenth century, and a few so late as the reign of Henry VIII. The walls of many of these edifices consist of a mixture of squared flints, inserted amidst a sort of frame-work of freestone, producing a firm and durable fabric, with the help of good cement. The use of flints was suggested by considerations of economy, as good stone could only be procured from distant quarries; but by careful practice, the workmen of former ages attained to a degree of perfection in the management of this rugged material, which may justly claim our admiration.

PLATE I. Fakenham Church is a large edifice, consisting of a nave and ailes, with a south porch, a chancel, and a lofty tower. The western entrance is here represented in an elevation and section, with a plan of part of the tower, to shew the position of the door-way. This church was erected in the fifteenth century, chiefly in the reign of Henry VI. The royal arms in one of the spandrils of the door, and the initial letter ℌ, surmounted by a crown, seem to refer to this monarch, whose memory was formerly honoured in Fakenham Church, by a light kept continually burning.*

PLATE II. shews one of the niches, or tabernacles, which stand on each side of the door. The ornaments of the canopies to these niches are particularly curious, and will be found so fully displayed on the Plate, as to require no farther elucidation. Both these niches are vacant; but they were evidently intended for the reception of statues, and perhaps were occupied by figures of the patron of the church, St. Peter, and his fellow-apostle, St. Paul, to whom the cross-keys and cross-swords, sculptured on shields over the door, may be supposed to allude.

* Henry Chichele, archbishop of Canterbury, was possessed of part of Fakenham, and probably contributed to the rebuilding of the church, as he was a munificent prelate, and a great patron of architecture. See the Account of his works at All Souls' College, Oxford, p. 6.

OXBOROUGH HALL, NORFOLK.

OXBOROUGH is situated in the south-west corner of the county of Norfolk, on the borders of the fens of Cambridgeshire.

The hall, or manor-house, was erected by Sir Edmund Bedingfield, knight, whose family had long been seated at a village of the same name in Suffolk, previous to the acquisition of Oxborough, by the marriage of Edmund Bedingfield with Margaret, daughter and coheiress of Sir Robt. de Tuddenham, knt. Sir Edmund was a zealous adherent of the house of York, and in high favour with King Edward IV., who granted him a license in 1482 to build towers and other fortifications at his manor of Oxborough, according to his own pleasure. From this time Oxborough Hall has continued to be the chief seat of the family, and is now in the possession of Sir Henry Bedingfield, Baronet.

This mansion is constructed of brick, and originally formed a quadrangle, measuring on the outside 171 feet from east to west, and rather less from north to south; with a court in the centre, 118 feet by 92 feet.* The hall occupied the middle of the southern range, and was a grand apartment, about 56 feet long and 29 feet broad, covered with an arched roof of timber, and furnished with two oriels or bay-windows at the upper end, and a screen at the lower,—in the usual fashion of the dining-halls of those times. The north porch of the hall opened into the court opposite to the principal entrance of the mansion, which occupies the middle of the north front. The whole south side of the quadrangle, including the hall, the great chamber or private dining-room, the great kitchen, and many other principal apartments, was taken down in the year 1778, when one side of the court was thrown open, and the arrangement of the remaining rooms altered.†

* See Plate IV., No. 3, which shews the entire plan, the gatehouse being distinguished by a black shade.

† Hengrave Hall, in Suffolk, another noble mansion of brick, erected by Sir Thomas Kitson, knight, under a license from Henry VIII. and finished in 1538, was reduced in size about the same time as Oxborough Hall; but the *hall* is yet standing at Hengrave, and the buildings completely surround an inner court, which is much smaller than that at Oxborough.—See "The History and Antiquities of Hengrave," published in 4to, 1822; an elegant and valuable work, compiled by John Gage, Esq. F.S.A., uncle to Sir Thos. Gage, to whom the place at present belongs.

Before this reduction, Oxborough Hall exhibited a complete example of an embattled mansion of the first class, a description of building which succeeded to the castles of earlier times,—being planned with more regard to internal space and convenience, but retaining sufficient strength to resist any casual assault of a hostile party. The style of the building has been compared to that of Queen's College, Cambridge, completed about the same time, and built of similar materials.* The whole structure was surrounded by a moat about 52 feet broad, and ten feet deep, supplied with water by a small brook; and the entrance was protected by a stately tower, one of the noblest specimens of the domestic architecture of the fifteenth century, which fortunately remains in a very perfect state, and forms the subject of the following Plates.†

PLATE I.—ELEVATION AND SECTION OF THE NORTH FRONT OF THE ENTRANCE TOWER.

The outward front of this stately pile is distinguished by two octangular turrets, standing forward with a deep and bold projection, and rising immediately from the moat, to the height of almost 80 feet, producing a very striking effect when viewed in perspective.‡ The approach to the gates at present is by a bridge of three arches; but originally a draw-bridge is supposed to have crossed the moat. The turret on the right hand is occupied by a spiral flight of steps, arched and constructed entirely with brick, and lighted by loop-holes in form of quatrefoils. The other turret contains four closets or small rooms, of which the one on the ground-floor has only narrow loop-holes, but the two next above it are lighted by small windows of a very neat form, one in each face of the turret. The two large windows over the

---

* This college was founded by Margaret of Anjou, the intrepid consort of Henry VI., the first stone being laid in 1448. The troubles of her husband's unfortunate reign prevented the foundress from completing the college; but her design was adopted by Elizabeth, the queen of Edward IV., and by her assistance, and the contributions of other benefactors, the whole was finished within about forty years from the foundation. Queen's College was constructed of brick, with a tower over the chief entrance; but the apartments have been mostly altered or rebuilt.

† The rector's mansion at Hadleigh, in Suffolk, has a turreted gatehouse, built of brick in a similar style to this, but of inferior elevation. It was erected by Dr. William Pykenham, archdeacon of Suffolk, chancellor to the Bishop of Norwich, and rector of the church of Hadleigh. He also built a stately residence for himself and his successors, the archdeacons of Suffolk, at Ipswich, in 1471; and an alms-house at Hadleigh in 1497.

‡ See "Lithographic Views illustrative of the Examples of Gothic Architecture."

gate give light to the principal chambers; and the arch above the uppermost window supports the parapet, which is detached from the main wall, apparently for the purpose of a machicollation.* In the square turret attached to the eastern side of the main building, is a secret recess or cell, just large enough for a man to stand up or lie down in it. The entrance is concealed by a trap-door in the pavement of a closet over it, so ingeniously contrived as not to be visible when shut. This place was undoubtedly made for the occasional retreat of a priest, during the persecution carried on under the penal laws against Catholics. Another such secret closet is said to have been found under a chimney, when the rooms on the opposite side of the court were pulled down.†

PLATE II.—OCTANGULAR TURRET ON THE SOUTH-EAST ANGLE OF THE TOWER.

The quoins of the tower, on the side next to the court, are plain and square, as high as the setting on of the parapet, where two turrets are placed, of similar plan to those on the outside, but of much smaller size. An elevation of one of these turrets is here delineated, together with part of the adjoining parapet and battlements; of which a section is also given. The plan is taken at the line marked B, shewing the breadth of the cruciform loop-holes, intended for reconnoitring or shooting at an assailant. A part of the corbels and little arches, which support the parapet at A, has been also drawn on a large scale, with a corresponding section. In all these details a careful regard to consistency of style is observable, nothing being left imperfect or unfinished; and the design of the battlements is particularly remarkable for its elegance. The square openings between the corbels, and in the panels of the turrets, seem to have been no more than scaffold-holes, made for the use of the builders, but so placed as to become ornamental.

* See the explanation of *Machecoulis*, in the Glossary appended to the "Specimens of Gothic Architecture."

† The houses of Catholic families were commonly provided with several such hiding-places, in which a priest might be concealed during any sudden visit from the officers called *poursuivants*, who used frequently to harass them with rigorous searches. Many of these were constructed by a religious man named John Owen, or "Little John," who, being apprehended in the year 1606, was so cruelly racked in the Tower of London, that he died in a short time after he was taken from the torture.—See "Challoner's Memoirs of Missionary Priests," 2 vols. 8vo, 1742; reprinted at Manchester, 1803; an authentic and most curious piece of history. Charles II. was hidden in such secret closets at Boscobel and Moseley, in Staffordshire, after the fatal battle of Worcester, A.D. 1651, when his life was saved by the care of F. Huddlestone.

PLATE III.—SECTION AND TWO PLANS OF THE ENTRANCE TOWER.

No. 1. This section passes through the centre of the inner and outer gateways, shewing the thickness of the walls, and the projection of the turrets, &c.

No. 2. The ground-plan gives the dimensions of the central passage, and the porters' lodges on each side of it; together with the forms of the ceilings, which are arched with brick-work, and decorated with ribs.

No. 3. Is a plan of the chamber on the first floor, which is a spacious room of very interesting appearance, being preserved in its original state, and retaining the name of "The King's Chamber." In this apartment King Henry VII. is said to have lodged, when on a visit to Sir Henry Bedingfield, to whom he granted three manors in Yorkshire, in reward of his faithful service against the rebels who were defeated at the battle of Stoke, near Newark-upon-Trent, in June, A.D. 1487. The floor is paved with small bricks, the ceiling is divided into squares by moulded oaken beams, and the walls are hung with fine old tapestry.

PLATE IV.—ELEVATION OF THE SOUTH FRONT OF THE ENTRANCE TOWER, WITH TWO PLANS.

Fig. 1. The inner front possesses little of that bold and castellated appearance which distinguishes the outside; the flat wall being only relieved by two semi-octagonal turrets, which serve as bay-windows to the porters' lodges, and the large chambers above them. The projection of these bay-windows is shewn in a plan placed beneath the elevation.

Fig. 2. gives a plan of the roof, with the battlements, turrets, and chimneys. The shafts of the chimneys were octagonal, and set in pairs on each side, but have been cut off just above the base mouldings, being the only parts that are wanting to complete the design.

Fig. 3. The plan of the whole structure, which has been already noticed in the general description of the house.

PLATE V.—DETAILS OF ORNAMENTAL PARTS IN THE NORTH FRONT.

No. 1. Quatre-foil ocillet, or loop-hole, in one of the turrets, with the arched panel in which it is recessed.

No. 2. Section of the same.

No. 3. Loop-hole in form of a cross.

No. 4. Section of the same. These loop-holes were so placed in the sides of the eastern turret as to overlook the immediate approach to the gates, and by this means the porter might examine strangers before he gave them admittance.

No. 5. Section of mouldings in the arch of the gateway.

No. 6. Elevation of part of the window of the lower chamber.

A. Section of a mullion and jamb of the same window.

B. Section of mullions in the head of one of the lower lights.

The general form of this window is very nearly square, and is simple, and well adapted to domestic architecture. The rising of the two little arches in the middle of the window, above those in the two outside lights, produces a pleasing effect. The upper window is smaller than this, but corresponds to it in the general style.

WOLTERTON, or EAST BASHAM, HALL, NORFOLK.

It is much to be regretted that this curious fabric should have fallen into ruins before any complete description, or representation, of it had been made; for it exhibits an extraordinary specimen of skilful workmanship in brick.* The words of the poet, "materiam superabat opus," may be truly spoken of it. Blomefield, the historian of Norfolk, found East Basham Hall "very much decayed and ruinous" when he visited it, about a century ago; and since that time it has suffered so much farther decay, that more than half of the house is now roofless, and reduced to broken walls, while the other part, though still kept in a habitable state, has been defaced and mutilated is such a manner that its original form cannot be exactly made out.

* Wolterton Hall, as it is sometimes called, from the name of the manor in which it stands, within the parish of East Basham or Barsham, was brought into public notice by a plan and some views published in the "Vetusta Monumenta," vol. iv. from drawings made by John Adey Repton, F.S.A., in 1808, with a descriptive account. Two other views, with a short account, were published about the same time in Britton's "Architectural Antiquities," vol. ii. It has since been regarded as one of the richest examples of ornamented brick-work in the kingdom, and some of its details have been copied in more than one modern mansion.

The building appears to have been begun by Sir Henry Fermor, Knt. in the reign of Henry VII., after he had become possessed of the manor by marriage with an heiress of the family of Wode, or Wood. Sir William Fermor carried on the work begun by his father, and completed it in the reign of Henry VIII.; but, from a date observed by Blomefield, it would seem that nearly forty years elapsed before the whole was finished. If this supposition be true, an older mansion probably stood on the same ground, which was pulled down by parts, and gradually rebuilt; and that might occasion the irregularity of the present structure. The founder's family continued in possession of the house above a century after its erection; when, in the reign of Charles I., it descended to that of Calthorpe. Sir Christopher Calthorpe, Knight of the Bath, resided here in the reign of Charles II.; but, by the failure of male issue, another change of proprietors took place, and East Basham passed to two co-heiresses, of whom Anne, daughter of Sir Christopher Calthorpe, was married to Sir Thomas L'Estrange of Hunstanton, Bart., and Elizabeth died unmarried. From this period, the house probably became neglected, and fell into decay; for Sir Thomas L'Estrange continued to reside at his paternal mansion* after he had become possessed of the whole property of East Basham. The family of L'Estrange being extinct on the death of Sir Henry, the last baronet, in 1760, Sir Jacob Astley, Bart., of Melton Constable, inherited East Basham through a marriage with Lucy, daughter to Sir Nicholas, and sister to Sir Thomas L'Estrange; and so it has descended to Sir Jacob Astley, Bart. the present possessor.

East Basham is situated between the towns of Walsingham and Fakenham, about ten miles from the sea-coast. The house stood very comfortably, with its front towards the south, and was well sheltered at the back by hills. The architecture was of a style purely domestic, without any pretensions to the character of a castle;† nevertheless, it must have been a stately and

* Hunstanton Hall, in the same county, which had for many centuries been the seat of the family of L'Estrange, has yielded in its turn to a similar fate with that of East Basham, and is going to ruin. It has been a noble pile, of a quadrangular form, chiefly erected about the end of the fifteenth century.

† At present there are no traces of a moat; but that defence was so universally added to country mansions in ancient times, where the circumstances of the place would allow it, that probably there may have been one here, which was filled up and levelled after its protection was no longer deemed necessary.

commodious dwelling when perfect, and the beauty of its ornaments excites our regret that no better care has been taken for their preservation.

PLATE I.—The plan, though drawn on a very small scale, will explain the distribution of the principal rooms on the ground-floor, to which the names are attached with letters of reference. The elevation is intended to give an idea of the principal front as it originally existed; the parts that are actually destroyed being filled up in conformity with those that remain perfect. The whole line of the front extends to the length of 140 feet, and is irregularly divided into seven compartments, of which the porch forms the centre. The front door opened into the hall, which is totally ruined: it measured 41 feet by 22, and was covered by a flat ceiling, at the height of 16 feet. A passage from the lower end of the hall led to the kitchen and other rooms, which are now subdivided, and occupied as a farm-house; and at the upper end is a spacious chimney, which seems a variation from the usual plan of such apartments. On the south side is a square projection, lighted by a broad bay-window; and between this and the porch is another window, of smaller size. The rooms on the north side of the hall are pulled down to the ground, and very little remains standing of the parlour adjoining the west end, which measured about 23 feet by $21\frac{1}{2}$, and had a bay-window looking over a bowling-green, of which the recess was $9\frac{1}{2}$ feet wide, and $7\frac{1}{2}$ in projection. The front of this room has been demolished, but appears restored in the Plate, uniformly with that of the hall and adjoining parts. As the following Plates represent the principal portions of the building in detail, no more seems necessary to be added to the general description, than to observe that the walls were constructed with brick, of which material most of the mouldings and ornaments were very curiously formed, and the roofs were covered with tiles.*

PLATE II.—SOUTH FRONT OF THE GATE-HOUSE.

The principal front of the mansion was enclosed by a court, with a gate-house in the centre, opposite to the porch over the hall door. On each side of the gate-house was a range of narrow buildings, for a porter's lodge and other offices, of which the external walls were pierced with narrow loop-holes, four on each side, intended for defence, if necessary. These offices have been destroyed; but the gate-house is standing, and its place

* The roof over the parlour, beyond the great chimney at the west end of the hall, appears to have been flat, and covered with lead; but this may admit of doubt.

is marked in the general plan, A. A larger plan of the entrance is inserted in the Plate now under consideration. The elevation of the south side has been richly decorated, according to the latest fashion of the *Gothic* or *Pointed* style of architecture. Over the great arch are the royal arms of Henry VIII., with the proper supporters, a griffin and a lion, of a large size. On two smaller shields are the arms of Fermor, impaled with those of Stapleton and another family: and a third shield, over the chamber window, bears the arms of Fermor alone. On the sides of the entrance are statues nearly of the size of life, now so much broken that their forms are hardly to be distinguished. Blomefield calls them "*two wild men, or giants, as janitors, armed with clubs.*" These figures, as well as the king's arms and supporters, are carved in brick; but the jambs of the gate, and some other parts, are of chalk-stone. The rest of the materials are brick; the ornaments being cast in moulds, and then burnt. The elevation is here represented in a perfect state, though the turrets have been broken down, and the parapet much mutilated, but repaired a few years since in an inferior style of workmanship to the original.*

PLATE III.—NORTH FRONT OF THE GATE-HOUSE.

The inner front of the gate-house resembles the other in its general outlines, but has less of ornamental details. In the spandrils of the great arch are two shields bearing the arms of Fermor singly, and Fermor impaled with those of Knevet and other families.

These elevations display great elegance, and are perfectly free from that incongruous admixture with details of the Italian style, which is found in many buildings of the reign of Henry VIII. The roof of the gateway is not vaulted, but only covered by the floor of the chamber over it, which is approached by a staircase in a turret attached to the west side. The arch of the outward front was originally closed by a pair of gates, which have been taken away; but there was no portcullis, nor any other means of defence.

* The view of this gate-house, inserted in Britton's "Architectural Antiquities," vol. ii. p. 92, shews the mutilated state of the battlements and turrets in the year 1807: and the plates in "Vetusta Monumenta," vol. iv., do the same. Of the turrets only one remained standing on the gate-house; viz. that on the north-east angle: it is given at large in Plate VII. No. 2.

PLATE IV.—SOUTH PORCH OF EAST BASHAM HALL.

This porch forms the principal entrance to the house, the door opening directly into the hall. The date of its erection is fixed to a certain period, by the arms of King Henry VII., distinguished by the supporters, a griffin and a greyhound, and his badge, the portcullis.* A smaller shield, beneath the royal arms, is supported by an angel; and on two others, in the spandrils of the arch, are the arms of Fermor without any impalement. The elevation is here restored to its original appearance, although the upper parts have been much injured, and the roof reduced to a shed or lean-to. It is altogether of a good design, but seems rather at variance with the other details of the front in its arched window, and the high point of the arch in the doorway. The plan is shewn separately, and also some details of mouldings, &c. which are described on the Plate.

PLATE V.—BAY-WINDOW OF THE HALL, &c.

The hall of this mansion did not form a distinct *house*,† but was merely a spacious room, having other apartments over it, not distinguished externally from the general mass of building. On the south side was a spacious recess of an oblong plan, lighted by a bay-window, represented in this Plate. This window was richly embellished with stained glass, of which nothing now remains but the description recorded in Blomefield's "History of Norfolk." The Latin motto, "Audaces Fortuna juvat,"‡ was repeated several times on

---

* All the English sovereigns from Richard II., who was the first that added supporters to his arms, down to James I., who introduced the unicorn of Scotland as a companion to the lion of England, adopted different supporters. Henry VII. used a red dragon, the ensign of Cadwallader, the last king of the Britons, from whom he claimed descent; and a white greyhound, in right of his queen, Elizabeth of York, she being descended from the family of Nevile, to which it belonged. The portcullis was borne by him in right of his mother, who was of the house of Beaufort.

Henry VIII. supported his arms with a dragon and a greyhound, the same as his father had done, in the beginning of his reign; but afterwards laid aside the greyhound, and adopted a lion, which all the succeeding sovereigns have retained.

† The term *house* was formerly applied to any portion of a large building which had a separate roof, in which sense we find the word used in many old surveys. See the "GLOSSARY" appended to "Specimens of Gothic Architecture." In this sense the halls of Eltham and Croydon palaces formed *houses*.

‡ "Fortune favours the bold."

scrolls; and the following arms were emblazoned in the six lights, which make up the breadth of the window :—

Howard, Duke of Norfolk, quartering Brotherton.
Earl Warren, and Moubray, in a garter.
Percy Earl of Northumberland, with his quarterings; viz., Lucy, Poynings, Fitzpaine, Bryan, &c. in a garter.
Knevet, quartering Cromwell, Tatteshall, Clifton, Basset, &c.
Argent, on a pale sable, a conger's head, for Lucee or Gascoine.
Also, Barry of six argent and gules; and the date of 1538.*

The narrow window belonged to a closet that opened into the parlour, of which only a few fragments remain, barely sufficient to shew its dimensions.† The window above this gave light to another closet, and the larger window into a great chamber over the hall, which Blomefield calls the "nursery." This room was wainscoted with panels, on which were carved "heads of men and women in antique dresses;" and under the heads of one man and woman were the arms of Fermor and Wood, and under others Fermor and Knevet, Yelverton and Fermor, and Berney and Fermor.‡ All these decorations have long since perished, together with the roof and floor of the chamber. The ornamental frieze over the upper window is filled with the arms of Stapleton, a lion rampant, the royal badge of the rose, and male and female heads; all curiously moulded in brick. Similar ornaments appear

* Besides the arms here mentioned, Mr. Gough informs us, that, "In a window of this house were formerly the armorial pedigree and alliances of the family of Calthorpe, from the conquest to the middle of the last century (seventeenth), contained in between fifty and sixty diamond-shaped panes of painted glass, neatly executed. They are most of them entire, and are placed in a bow-window in the library of Sir John Fenn, at East Dereham, who married a lady descended from this family."—*Additions to* CAMDEN's *Britannia*, vol. ii. p. 196; 2d edition, 1806.

† The great parlour appears, from Blomefield's account, to have been richly decorated with carved work and painted glass. In the window were the arms of Fermor, impaled with those of the family of Wood, the preceding lords of the manor; viz., argent a saltire between four staples sable. Also Fermor impaling Stapleton; Berney impaling Fermor; Yelverton and Fermor. On the chimney-piece were the arms of Fermor impaling Knevet, with his quarterings; and also impaling Coote, &c., with this motto, "**Fortior est qui se, quam qui fortissima vincit.**" "He is a braver man who overcomes himself, than he who conquers the strongest towns." See the "Proverbs of Solomon," chap. xvi. v. 32, where the same sentiment is expressed in almost parallel terms.

On a piece of oak in the centre of the ceiling were carved the *quinque vulnera*, or five wounds of Christ, and round them this sentence, "**The Passion of God help me!**"

‡ These *antique heads* were probably of a similar description to some in the parsonage-house at Great Snoring.—(See the Plates.) Such grotesque portraits, generally in profile, were very fashionable among the decorations of architecture in the sixteenth century.

over the lower windows, placed alternately in panels. The turret, or buttress at the angle, is decorated with the like armorial bearings, and in the upper part with capital letters, all formed of moulded brick.*

PLATE VI.—The tower exhibited in this Plate forms the most striking feature of the whole house, and is a curious piece of architecture. It contains three rooms, of which the two lowest are covered with vaulted roofs of brick, ribbed and groined. The heights and other dimensions of these rooms are shewn in the section, which passes through the centre of the tower from front to back. The plan belongs to the second room, from which a spiral staircase, in the turret at the south-east angle, leads up to the third room, where there is a fire-place, shewn in the section. Undoubtedly this tower was intended for some important purpose, though it may not be easy to ascertain what that purpose was. The middle chamber might be constructed for the safe keeping of the family evidences, title-deeds, money, jewels, and other valuable effects, being strongly arched and floored with brick; and the upper room was probably a library or studying chamber.† The elevation of this tower above the surrounding buildings would also fit it for the use of keeping watch during the time of any disturbance in the country, and for setting up a beacon; these precautions being commonly practised even in later times than when East Basham Hall was built.‡

PLATE VII.—No. 1. gives an elevation of a turret at the east end of the south front, with a plan shewing its form and breadth in two different parts, and also the manner in which the bricks are put together.

---

* These letters are scattered over various parts of the house, among them we find H. R., for *Henricus Rex;* E. R., for *Elizabetha Regina;* also the letters B.M. P. V. T. &c.

† At the top of one of the towers of Wressil Castle, a seat of the Lord Percy, "was a Study caullid *Paradise.*"—LELAND's *Itinerary*, vol. i. fol. 59. At Leckinfield, another residence of the same nobleman, Leland also saw "a little studying Chaumber caullid Paradise." A chamber in the upper story of a tower at Stanton-Harcourt, county Oxon, formerly the residence of the ancient family of Harcourt, is still shewn to the admirers of Pope as the study in which he composed some books of his Homer.

‡ Hengrave Hall, Suffolk, a very fine specimen of contemporary architecture, had also a tower, which was pulled down, with some other parts, in 1775. Beacons were commonly set on the towers of churches, as well as on those of castles and mansions, so late as the reign of Queen Elizabeth.

No. 2. exhibits a similar turret on the north-east angle of the gate-house, with two plans corresponding to the elevation.*

These turrets, or pinnacles, for they may be called by either name, must have been highly ornamental to the building in a general view, though it may be questioned whether they were designed in accordance with good taste. They nearly resembled the tunnels of chimneys in shape and size, but wanted the character of usefulness which makes a chimney appear proper to a domestic edifice. The same objection may be extended to the octagonal buttresses which are attached to the quoins of the building: they are like turrets rather than buttresses, yet are too narrow to admit of any internal space, and therefore seem to possess no proper character either as turrets or buttresses. These observations are submitted to the consideration of architects, without any wish to put forth positive opinions on a question of taste.

PLATE VIII.—DETAILS OF THE SOUTH FRONT OF THE GATE-HOUSE.

No. 1. Elevation of part of the embattled parapet, and of the ornamental string-course under it, with a section of the same.

No. 2. Part of the frieze, or string-course, under the chamber-window.

No. 3. The springing of the arch over the gateway, on the left hand, with the canopy over the head of one of the "janitors."

No. 4. Two portions of one of the turrets are here given at large, shewing the forms and projections of the mouldings.

No. 5. The mouldings of the jambs, mullion, and sill of the window, are shewn above the figure 5; and beneath it the section, &c. of a jamb of the gateway.

All these details display an excellent taste.

PLATE IX.—ELEVATION AND PLAN OF A STACK OF CHIMNEYS.

These chimneys are built upon the western gable of the hall, to which two of the tunnels belonged; two others were appropriated to the chamber

---

* All the turrets of the house have been broken down to the bases of the upper parts, excepting one at the eastern angle of the front; but some of them have been replaced by substitutes of modern work. The original one is here represented; the others, of the larger size, are restored in the Plates, in conformity with it; and the smaller ones from that on the north-east angle of the gate-house, the only original one remaining out of four.

over the hall, two to the parlour, two to the chamber above it, and the other two to fire-places in the garrets.* Such a large group of chimneys is scarcely to be seen in any other building of this date, and the richness of their ornaments is quite extraordinary. Some of the projecting mouldings on the top have fallen to decay, but the other parts remain perfect.

PLATE X.—ORNAMENTS ON THE GREAT STACK OF CHIMNEYS.

The tunnels of these chimneys are of a cylindrical form, composed of tiles moulded for the purpose, the ornaments upon them displaying five different patterns, all of which are here given at large. The plinth on which the tunnels stand is adorned with the arms of Stapleton and Wood, the royal badge of the rose, and two busts, which perhaps were intended to represent King Henry VII. and his queen, Elizabeth of York.

PLATE XI.—DETAILS OF THE NORTH FRONT OF THE GATE-HOUSE, AND OTHER PARTS.

No. 1. represents the frieze, or string-course, in the middle of the north front of the gate-house.

No. 2. Cornice under the parapet of the tower in the south front of the house.—See Plate VI.

No. 3. Tracery in small panels on the turrets of the tower.—See Plate VII. No. 1.

No. 4. Frieze, or string-course, running along the middle of the south front.—(See Plate V.) The arms belonged to the families of Wood and Stapleton; and the spaces between the panels are charged with roses and heads alternately.

No. 5. One of the shields which decorate the spandrils of the north arch of the gate-house. The arms are those of Fermor with an impalement.

No. 6. A part of the tracery on a turret of the south front of the house is here given at large.—(See No. 1 in Plate VII.) The spaces between the mouldings are filled with roses and lions' heads formed of moulded tiles.

* The chimneys of halls, kitchens, and other apartments where large fires were wanted, had commonly two tunnels, and sometimes more. In the hall at Chillington there were no fewer than eight tunnels to one hearth.—PLOT's *Staffordshire*, p. 359.

PLATE XII.—DETAILS OF THE TOWER AND PORCH OF EAST BASHAM HALL.

No. 1. shews part of the window in the middle room of the tower.— See Plate VI.

No. 2. gives a part of the window in the lower room of the tower.

The mullions, jambs, &c. of these windows are composed of bricks.

No. 3. A portion of the mouldings and tracery in front of the middle story of the tower is here given at large. The position of these ornaments is shewn in the elevation on Plate VI., where the projection of the window, supported by the mouldings over the tracery, is also shewn in the section of the tower. The heads are similar to those on the great chimney and other parts of the house.

No. 4. shews one jamb of the doorway to the porch, with sections of the mouldings both in the arch and jamb, and the little columns on each side. See the elevation of the porch in Plate IV.

THORPLAND HALL, NORFOLK.

THORPLAND adjoins to East Basham, but is a hamlet of the town of Fakenham, from which it lies distant about two miles. Here was formerly a chapel, dedicated to St. Thomas, which was subject to the rectory of Fakenham, Thorpland being a member of the same parish. We learn from Blomefield's history that the manor belonged to the family of Fermor in the sixteenth century; and that, in the reign of Elizabeth, it was held in fee-farm of the Duchy of Lancaster, by Thomas Fermor, Esq. Thorpland, as well as East Basham, afterwards came into the possession of the Calthorpes; and some letters of Sir Christopher Calthorpe are dated from Thorpland Hall in the year 1680.

There can be very little doubt that Thorpland Hall was erected by some of the Fermors. It is evidently of the same date as East Basham Hall, and might be intended for the jointure-house of a widow, or the residence of a younger branch of the family. The inferiority of the house at Thorpland to that of East Basham puts all comparison out of question, excepting only the details. Still, it is a valuable example of its class, as it remains in a very perfect state, and exhibits several architectural members well suited to modern imitation.

Plate I.—Principal Front of Thorpland Hall.

The outlines of the front deviate but little from uniformity, although the porch is not exactly in the centre. The windows are rather irregular, but are all remarkably plain, being merely divided by mullions into square-headed compartments.* The eave of the roof seems to have lost its original finishing, for we can hardly suppose it to have been left in the naked form in which it is now seen. There is no appearance of there ever having been battlements, or a parapet; but there might be a cornice composed of plaster with curved ribs of wood, a common ornament to the roofs of houses of this style. The plain forms of the other parts are strongly contrasted with the style of the chimneys, on which the utmost pains have been expended, quite contrary to the practice of modern times. The walls of the house are composed of flints, with brick-work in the chimneys, quoins, &c., and stone in the window-frames.

Plate II.—Details of Chimneys, Gable, and other Parts.

No. 1. The tunnels of these chimneys are composed of moulded tiles, on each of which is impressed a lion rampant, probably in allusion to the arms of Stapleton, or the heraldic figure called the fleur-de-lis. A third variety of ornament was formed by a sort of trellis in lozenges; and different patterns occur on some other of the chimneys.

No. 2. The plan of the chimneys is here shewn at large, with the curves formed in their capitals, and the octagonal lines of their bases.

No. 3. One end of the house is here given entire, with a section of the chimneys and gable. The composition of this part is altogether good; the

---

* This plainness in the forms of windows became common in the middle of the sixteenth century, and was generally used during the reigns of Elizabeth and James I. In the earlier examples, each light had commonly a small arch in the head, which added much to the ornamental appearance of a window. At East Basham we find both these varieties, and their contrasted effects are very striking.

octagonal buttresses are remarkably neat; and the chimneys are beautiful. Fig. A. shews one of the pinnacles of the gable at large; the plan of the same is given at B; and a section of the coping at C.

PLATE III.—FRONT PORCH OF THORPLAND HALL.

No. 1. Elevation of the door and the lower part of the porch, over which is a small chamber.

No. 2. Section of the same, taken in the centre, through the whole projection, shewing one of the benches on the sides.

No. 3. Plan of the porch.

The door is hung in a massy frame of oak, moulded in a corresponding style with the masonry. The original door remains unaltered, and retains the old knocker and handle. The door itself is quite plain.

No. 4. gives the plan of one jamb of the front arch, and an elevation of the same, as it appears within the doorway.

All these details are worthy of examination, in order to a complete knowledge of our old domestic architecture, of which the remains are every day growing more and more rare.

THE PARSONAGE-HOUSE,

AT GREAT SNORING, NORFOLK.

THIS village of Great Snoring is situated in the immediate vicinity of East Basham and Thorpland, and exhibits another remarkable piece of ancient domestic architecture, in the rectory, or parsonage-house, here represented. The peculiar style of the building shews it to have been erected in the reign of Henry VIII.; and from the *shells and tuns* carved on the windows and other parts, we may infer that its founder was of the family of Shelton, such quaint devices being often seen in buildings of that period.

The manor of Snoring came into the possession of Sir Ralph Shelton, of Shelton, in Norfolk, on the death of his cousin, Hugh de Burgolyon, in the reign of Edward III. It continued in the same family until the year

1611, when Sir Ralph Shelton sold the lordship to Thomas Richardson, sergeant-at-law, and afterwards lord chief justice of the King's Bench. This Sir Ralph Shelton was killed at the Isle of Rhé, in France, A.D. 1628; and leaving no issue, his family became extinct.

PLATE I.—SOUTH FRONT, WINDOW, AND DETAILS OF ORNAMENTS.

This curious structure being mutilated and altered in different parts, much of its original design cannot be made out. The elevation represents the south front, with a turret at the south-east angle; beyond which another line of front extends towards a second turret. The ruins of one or two other turrets are said to have been visible within memory, but these are now entirely obliterated. The two fronts do not stand at a right angle, but obliquely, as if the building, when complete, had formed a polygon of five sides; but whether this singular plan was actually executed or not, it is now impossible to discover. The walls of this house are constructed of brick, and the ornaments are formed of tiles, very curiously moulded and fitted to their respective situations. The first and second stories are distinguished by friezes, somewhat similar to those on the front of East Barsham Hall, though differently ornamented. The upper parts of the turrets are covered with tracery of very elegant style; but, unfortunately, they both have lost their original terminations, so that it cannot be determined whether they had spires, pinnacles, or battlements, on the top. The chimney has been broken off, and afterwards rebuilt in a plain manner; and the door and lower windows are blocked up. The windows of the chamber story are remarkably handsome, though of very moderate dimensions. One of them is shewn at large in Fig. 2. The jambs and head are ornamented with a hollow moulding, studded with *shells* and *tuns* placed alternately, forming a rebus on the name of Shelton.

Fig. 3. A portion of the upper frieze is here displayed at large, with a section of the mouldings. In this frieze, the heads, and the ornaments around them, partake of Italian taste. The larger portraits only exhibit profiles of a man and woman, many times repeated. The string-courses, above and below these heads, are filled with very small and delicate ornaments.[*]

---

[*] The "antique heads" described by Mr. Blomefield in one of the rooms of East Barsham Hall probably were of this description.—See page 54.

PLATE II.—DOOR, AND OTHER DETAILS.

No. 1. This door is a very curious piece of workmanship, evidently of a date coeval with the architecture of the house. The panels are all richly carved, the small one in the centre bearing the shell and tun, in allusion to the founder's name; with 𝕴𝖍𝖈 on one side, and 𝕸𝖆 conjoined on the other, the abbreviations of Jesus and Mary; shewing it to be of earlier date than the change of religion.*

No. 2. One of the small niches at the angles of the turret is here shewn at large, with horizontal sections taken at different heights.

No. 3. Tracery on the turret, in the lower compartment, with the mouldings at the bottom of the panels.

No. 4. Tracery in the upper part of the turret.

No. 5. Part of the frieze surrounding the turret, with a section of the same.†

The string-course above the panels is similar to that on the bottom of the upper frieze, the hollow moulding being filled with small shields, each charged with a cross, and supported by two dogs. The bottom string-course bears the letters 𝕴𝖍𝖈 and 𝕸𝖆, similar to those on the door.

No. 6. gives the panels on the base of the chimney, and a section of the string-course over them, at large.

* The larger panels are carved in nearly the same pattern as some in the room of Beddington Manor House, Surrey, the ancient seat of the Carew family.—See Pugin's "Gothic Ornaments." There is also a resemblance to the tracery on the outward front of the gate-house at East Basham, above the chamber window.

† The lower frieze at East Basham is of similar style to this, but does not extend across the turrets or buttresses of the front.—See Plates I. V. &c.

INDEX.

A

All Souls' College, Oxford, account of, 6, 7, 8; with four Plates.
  I. ――― entrance, 7; pl. x.
  II. ――― chapel, 7; pl. xii.
  III. ――― groined roof, 8; pl. xi.
  IV. ――― stalls, tracery of, 8; pl. xiii.
Armorial devices at Magdalen College, 13, 14.
――― at Beddington Hall, 25.
――― at Croydon Palace, 28, 29.
――― at Eltham Palace, 37, 40.
Arms in the bay-window of Balliol College, 4.
――― on Magdalen College Chapel, 13.
――― at Brazennose College, 19.
――― in Beddington Church, 25.
――― in ditto Manor House, 25.
――― in Croydon Palace, 28, 29.
――― at East Basham Hall, 53, 54, 57.
――― at Thorpland Hall, 59.

B

Balliol College, Oxford, account of, 4, 5; with two Plates.
  I. ――― oriel-window, 5; pl. vi.
  II. ――― ditto, 5; pl. vii.
Basham Hall; see Wolterton.
Beddington Church, Surrey, account of, with two Plates, 24.
  I. ――― screen in the chancel, 24; pl. xxxv.
  II. ――― tomb of Sir Richard Carew, 24; pl. xxxvi.

Beddington Manor House, account of, 25.
――― curious lock, 25, 26; pl. xxxvii.
Bells of Merton College, 2.‡

C

Chichelé, Archbp. notices of his life and works, 6.
Chimney, curious, at Magdalen College, Oxford, 15.
――― with ten tunnels, at East Basham Hall, 56, 57.
――― at Thorpland Hall, 59.
――― in halls and kitchens, 57.*
Cloisters of New College, Oxford, 5.
Crosby Hall, London, 38, 39.
Croydon Palace, Surrey, account of, with three Plates, 26, 27, 28, 29.
  I. ――― section of the hall, 27, 28; pl. xxxviii.
  II. ――― ditto, and details, 28; pl. xxxix.
  III. ――― bay-window, 29; pl. xl.
Chapel of Croydon Palace, account of, with two Plates, 29, 30.
  I. ――― section and plan, 30.
  II. ――― details and section, 30.
Chestnut timber, 41.†
Closets, for concealing priests, in the mansions of Catholic families, 47.†
Christian Architecture, a new term, xviii.

D

Domestic architecture, the *Early Pointed*, or *Lancet* style, ill adapted to it, x.

INDEX.

E

Epitaph of Sir Richard Carew, 24.
English Architecture, a term improperly applied, xvi.

F

Fakenham Church, Norfolk, account of, with two Plates, 44.
  I. ———— western door, 44; pl. l.
  II. ———— niche, and details, 44; pl. li.
Fires, manner of placing them in ancient halls, 37.
Folded scrolls, or drapery, carved on panels; temp. Hen. VIII., 23.

G

Glass, stained, in Merton College Chapel, 3.
————, formerly at East Basham Hall, Norfolk, 53, 54.
Gothic architecture, defects of modern practice, xii.
———— in France and Germany, xvi. xvii.
————, usage of the term *Gothic* justified, xvii.||

H

Hadleigh, Suffolk, tower, 46.†
Halls, dimensions of several, 36.‡
Height of domestic buildings before the reign of Queen Elizabeth, 16.
House, a term used for part of any large building, 53.†
Hengrave Hall, Suffolk, 45.

I

Inigo Jones, his incompetence in Gothic architecture, xiv.
———— employed at St. John's College, Oxford, 9.*
Inscription on a door in St. Alban's Abbey, 23.
———— on a tomb at Beddington, 24.
———— in the hall of Croydon Palace, 28.
———— in East Basham Hall, 53, 54.
Irregularity of ancient buildings, 17.

K

King, Edward, Esq. allusion to, 35.†

L

Label, or hood-mould, term used by the old masons, 14.*
Langley, B., author of a work on Gothic architecture, xii.*
Loop-holes at Oxborough Hall, 48; pl. lvi.

M

Magdalen College, Oxford, account of, 10, 11, 12; with ten Plates, viz.
———— entrance, title-page.
  I. ———— porch of the chapel, 12; pl. xvii.
  II. ———— sections of ditto, 13; pl. xviii.
  III. ———— details of ditto, 13; pl. xix.
  IV. ———— part of the chapel, 14; pl. xx.
  V. ———— chimney and turret, 15; pl. xxi.
  VI. ———— oriel-window, 15; pl. xxii.
  VII. ———— entrance tower, 16, 17; pl. xxiii. and xxiv.
  VII., VIII. details of ditto, 17, 18; pl. xxv.
  IX. ———— Mouldings, &c. 18; pl. xxvi.
Merton College, Oxford, account of, 1, 2; with four Plates, viz.
  I. ———— part of the chapel, 2, 3; pl. ii.
  II. ———— north doorway, 3; pl. iii.
  III. ———— stained glass, 3; pl. iv.
  IV. ———— part of chancel, 3, 4; pl. v.
Merton College Chapel, tracery on the ancient stalls, 10; pl. xvi. No. 2.

N

New College, Oxford, account of, 5; with two Plates; viz.
  I. ———— part of cloisters, 5, 6; pl. viii.
  II. ———— details of the chapel, 6; pl. ix.

O

Oxborough Hall, Norfolk, description of, with five Plates, 45–49.
  I. ———— outward front, 46; pl. lii.

INDEX.

II. Oxborough Hall, turret and details, 47 ; pl. liii.
III. ——— section and plans, 48 ; pl. liv.
IV. ——— inward front, 48 ; pl. lv.
V. ——— window, and details, 49 ; pl. lvi.

P

Pendent spandrils in vaulted roofs, notices of some, 9.*
Pendents in the roof of Eltham Hall, 41.
Pews in churches, ill effects of, 12.
Plaster, modern use of, instead of stone, 8, 15.
——— instead of oak, 43.
Pointed arches, *compound* and *simple*, defined, 39.
Porch, original purposes of, when attached to a church, 21.
Purgatory, sculpture of, at All Souls' College, 7.

R

Rebus on the name of Shelton, 60, 62.
Richmond Palace, notice of, 36.†
Roof of All Souls' College Chapel, 7.
——— of Magdalen College Chapel, 15.
——— of Eltham Palace Hall described, 39, 40, 41.
——— of Oxborough Hall, destroyed, 45.

S

St. Alban's Abbey, Herts, account of ; with one Plate, 23.
——— doors of chapels, 23 ; pl. xxxiv.
St. John's College, Oxford, account of, 8, 9 ; with three Plates : viz.
I. ——— entrance tower, 9 ; pl. xiv.
II. ——— vaulted roof, 9, 10 ; pl. xv.
III. ——— tracery of doors, 10 ; pl. xvi.
St. Katharine's Hospital, London, account of, 22, 23 ; with one Plate.
——— canopy of a stall, 22, 23 ; pl. xxxiii.
St. Mary's Church, Oxford, account of, 21 ; with three Plates.
I. ——— part of the nave, 21 ; pl. xxx.
II. ——— parts of the choir, 21 ; pl. xxxi.
III. ——— stalls in the choir, 22 ; pl. xxxii.

St. Peter's in the East, Oxford, account of that church, 19, 20 ; with two Plates.
I. ——— south porch, 20 ; pl. xxviii.
II. ——— section, and plan, 20, 21 ; pl. xxix.
Snoring, Great, Norfolk, account of the Parsonage-House, 60, 61, 62 ; with two Plates.
I. ——— south front, 61 ; pl. lxxii.
II. ——— details of ornament, 62 ; pl. lxxiii.
Statues at All Souls' College, Oxford, 7.
— ——— at Magdalen College, 12, 13, 17.
— ——— at East Basham Hall, 52.
Supporters of the King's arms, different, 53.†

T

Thorpland Hall, Norfolk, account of, 58, 59, 60, with three Plates.
I. ——— front elevation, 49 ; pl. lxix.
II. ——— gable and chimneys, 59, 60 ; pl. lxx.
III. ——— front porch, 60 ; pl. lxxi.
Tower in East Basham Hall, 55.

V

Vaulted roof at All Souls' College, 8.
——— at St. John's College, 9.
——— of the bay-windows of Eltham Palace Hall, 37. 38.
——— in the tower of East Basham Hall, 55.

W

Walsingham, Old, Norfolk, description of seats in the church of, 42, 43 ; with a Plate.
——— carved oak seat, pl. xlviii.
Walsingham, New, description of a ceiling in the church of, 43 ; with a Plate.
——— oak ceiling, pl. xlix.
Waynflete, William of, notices of his life and works, 10, 11, 12.
Westminster Hall, comparison of its roof with that of Eltham, 39.
Window, bay or oriel, in Balliol College, 4 ; ditto, in Magdalen College, 15 ; ditto, in Croydon

INDEX.

Palace. 29 ; ditto, in Eltham Palace, 38, 39 ; ditto, in East Basham Hall, 53 ; ditto, with plain, square heads, 59.*

Wolterton, or East Basham Hall, Norfolk, account of. 49–58 ; with twelve Plates.

I. ———— south front, 51 ; pl. lvii.
II. ———— south front of gate-house, 51 ; pl. lviii.
III. ———— north front of ditto, 52 ; pl. lix.
IV. ———— south porch, 53 ; pl. lx.
V. Wolterton Hall, bay-window, 53, 54; pl. lxi.
VI. ———— tower, 55 ; pl. lxii.
VII. ———— turrets, 55, 56 ; pl. lxiii.
VIII. ———— details, 56 ; pl. lxiv.
IX. ———— chimneys, 56, 57 ; pl. lxv.
X. ———— details of chimneys, 57 ; pl. lxvi.
XI. ———— mouldings, and details, 57; pl. lxvii.
XII. ———— windows, doors, &c. 58 ; pl. lxviii.

Wykeham, William of, Bishop of Winchester, notices of his life and works, 5.

THE END.

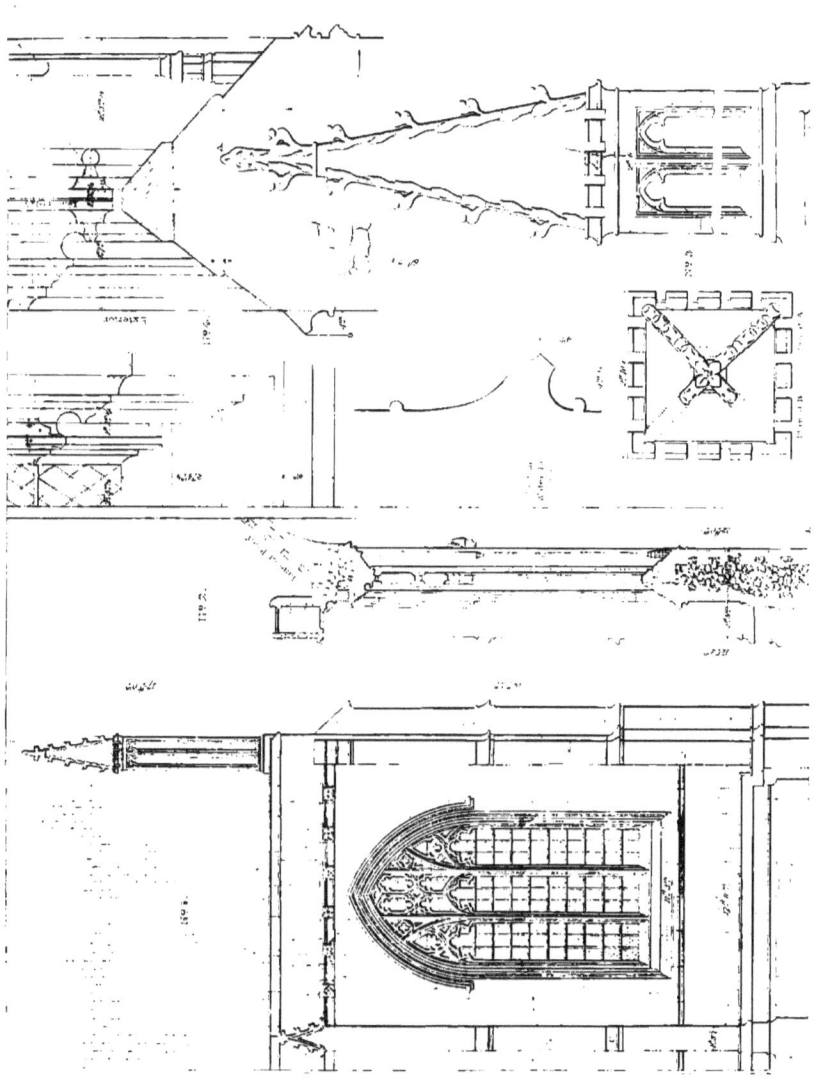

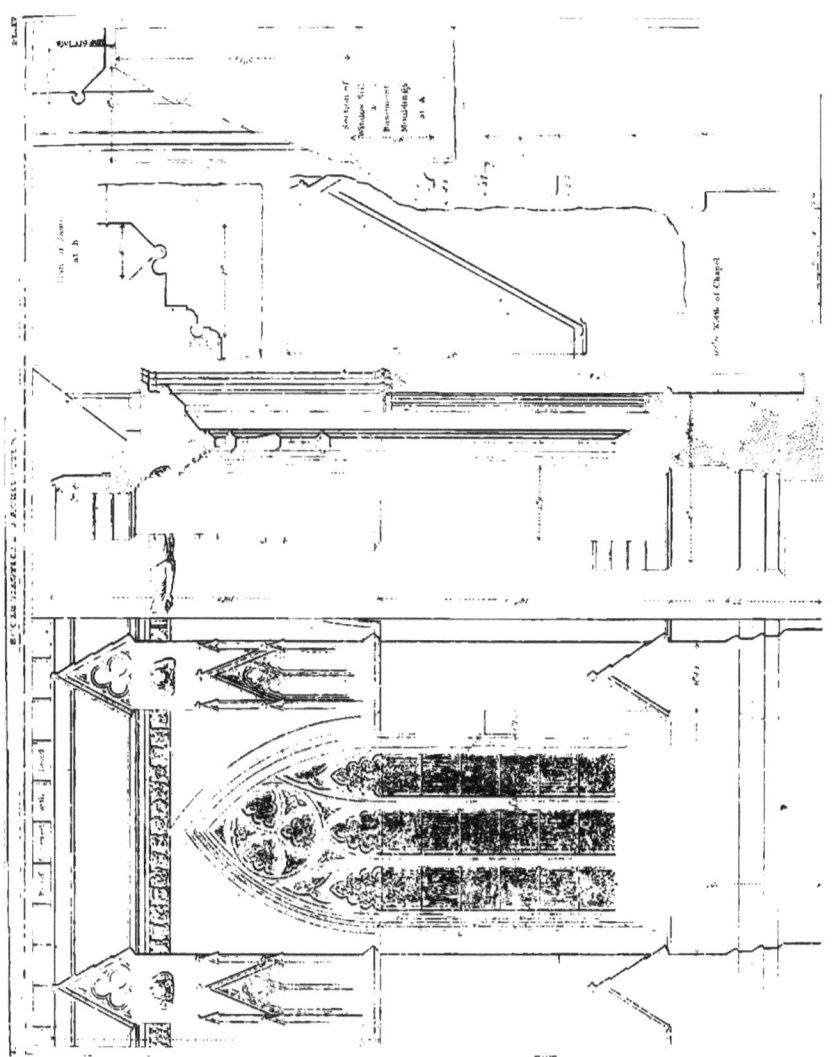

DOMESTIC ARCHITECTURE.

altered by the late James Wyatt

A. Pugin Arch. del.

COLLEGIATE ARCHITECTURE.

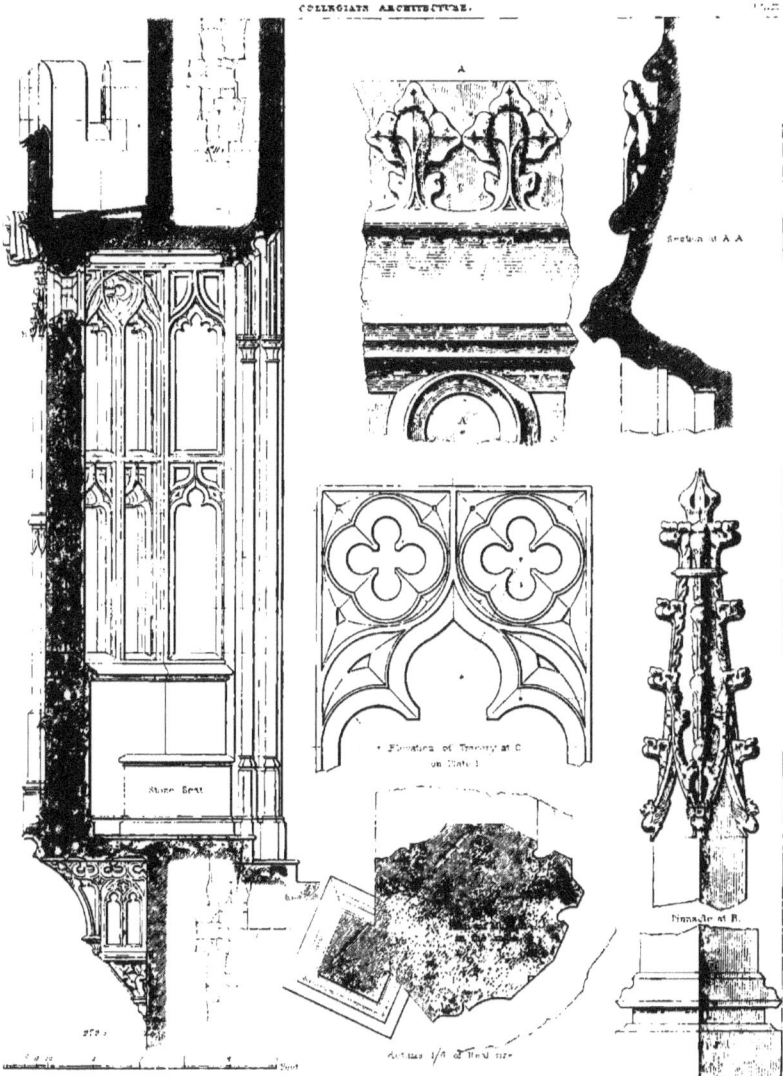

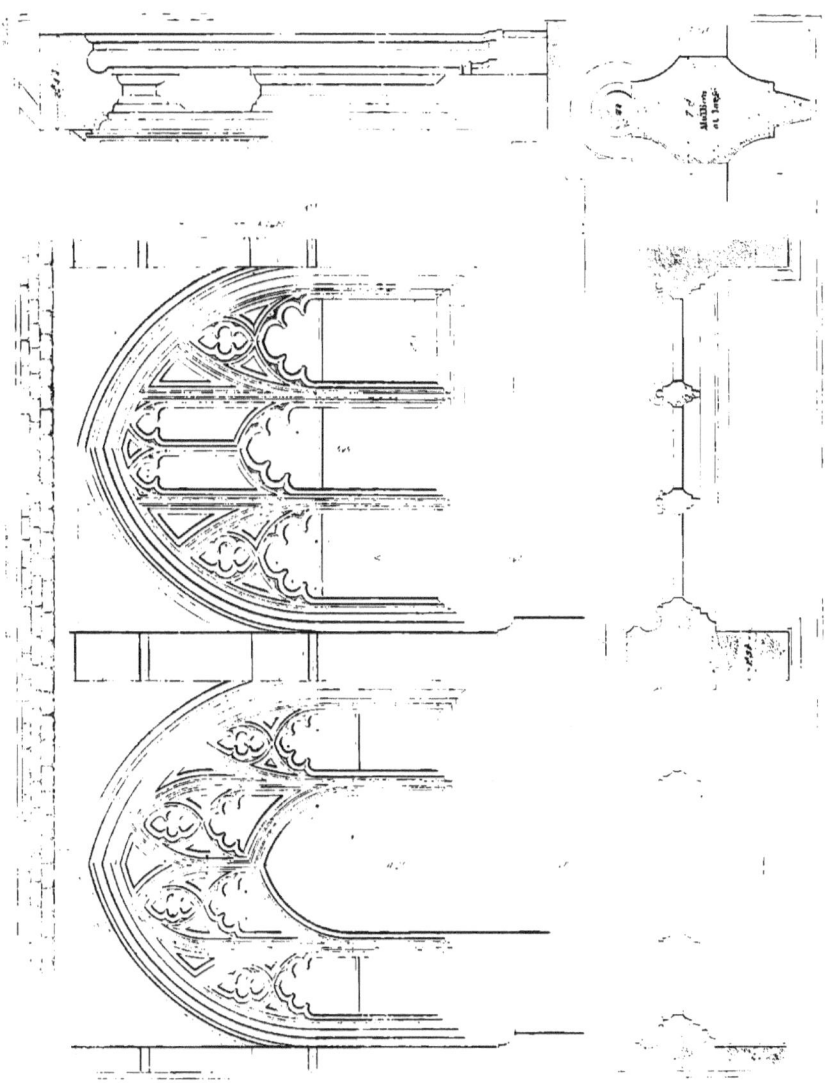

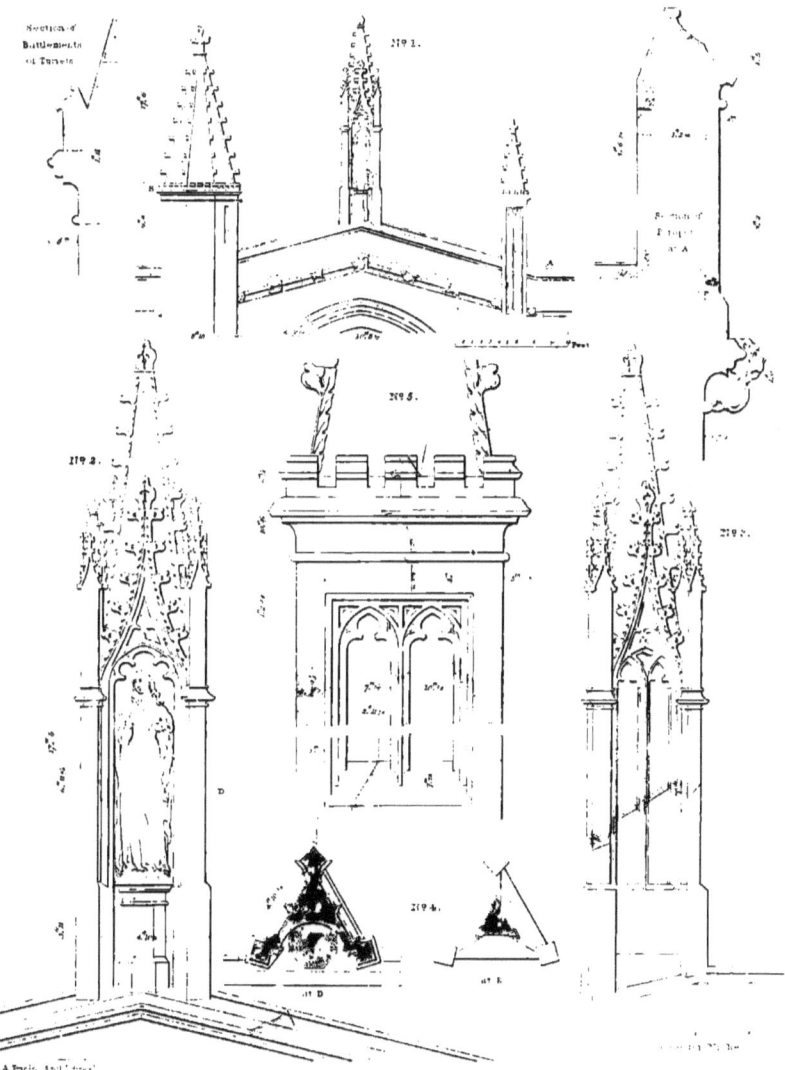

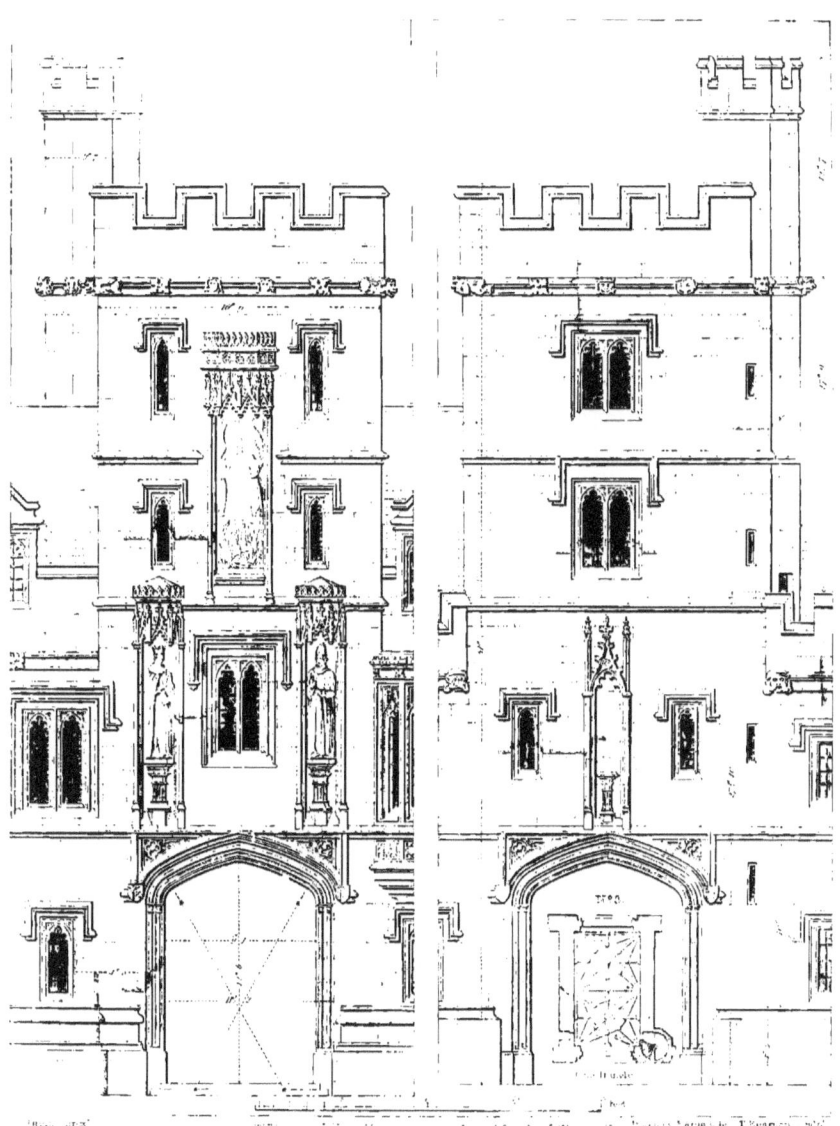

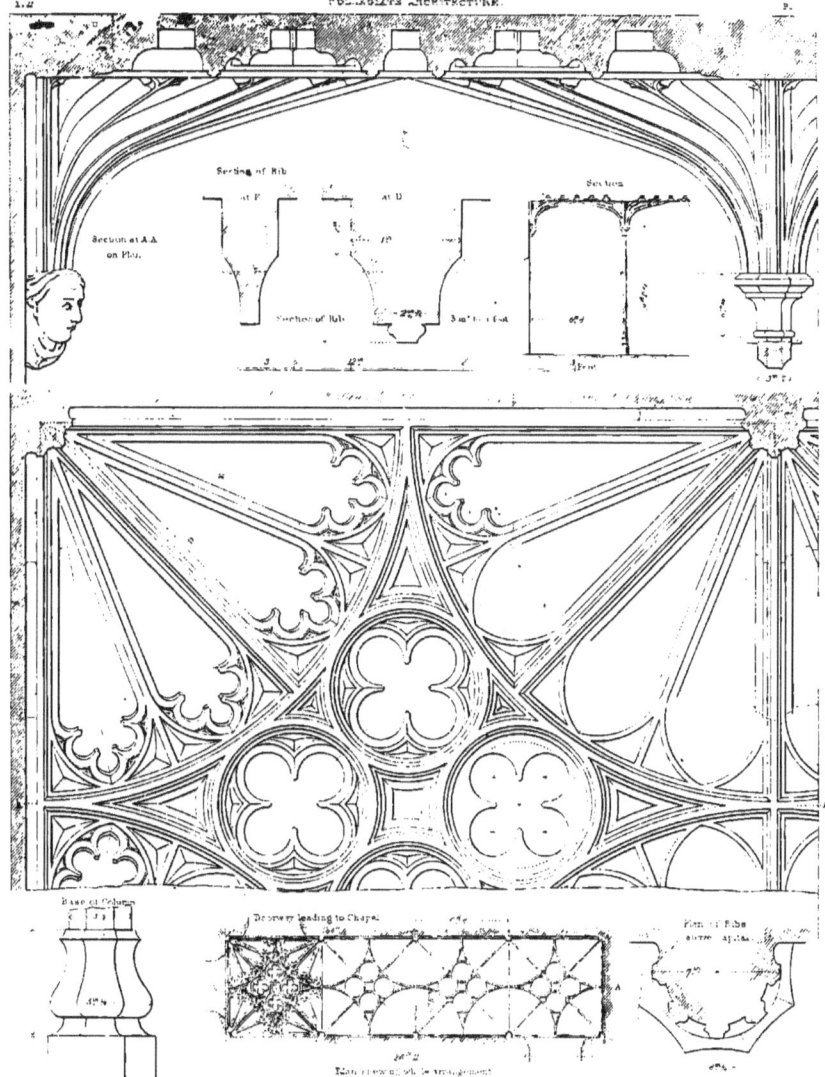

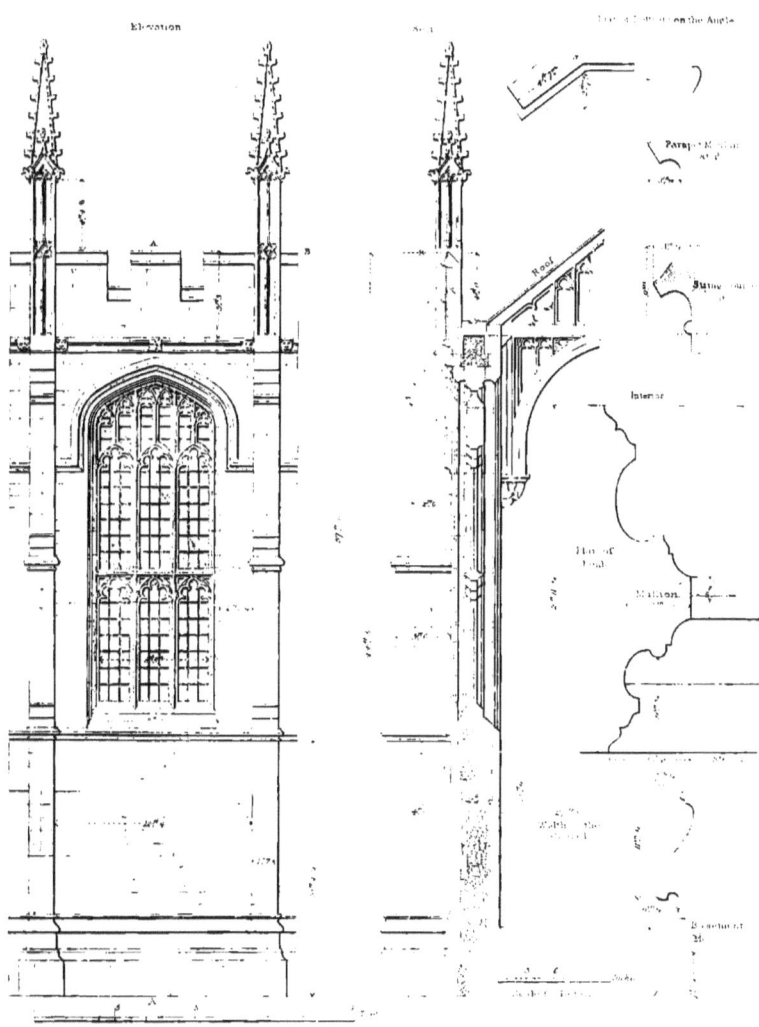

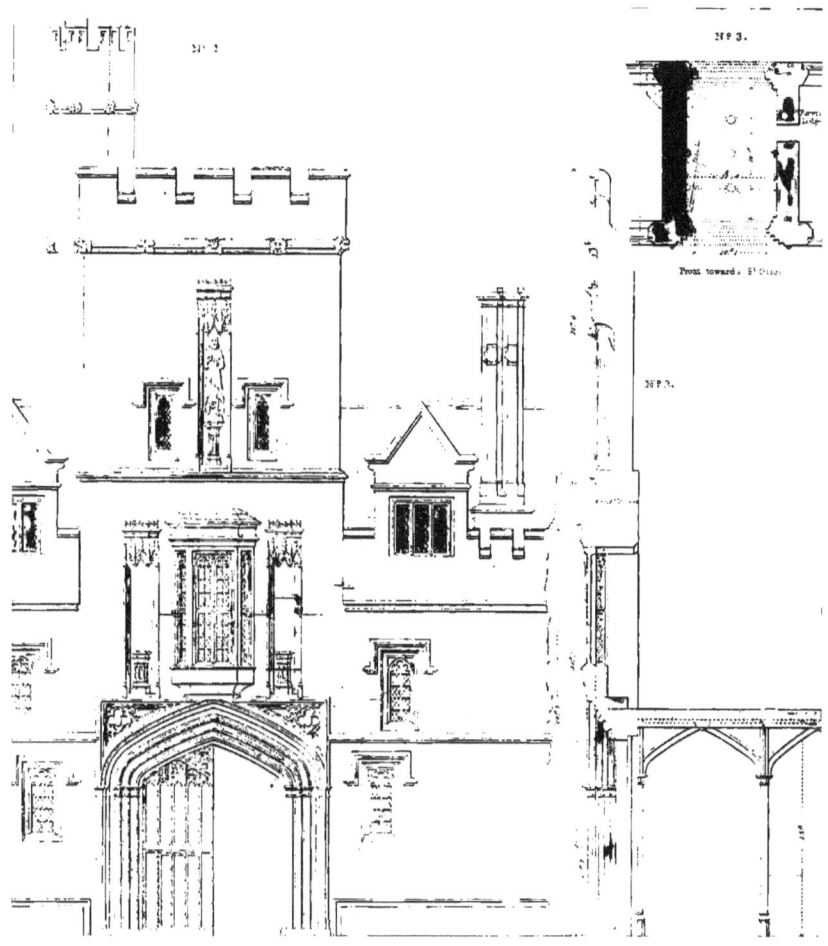

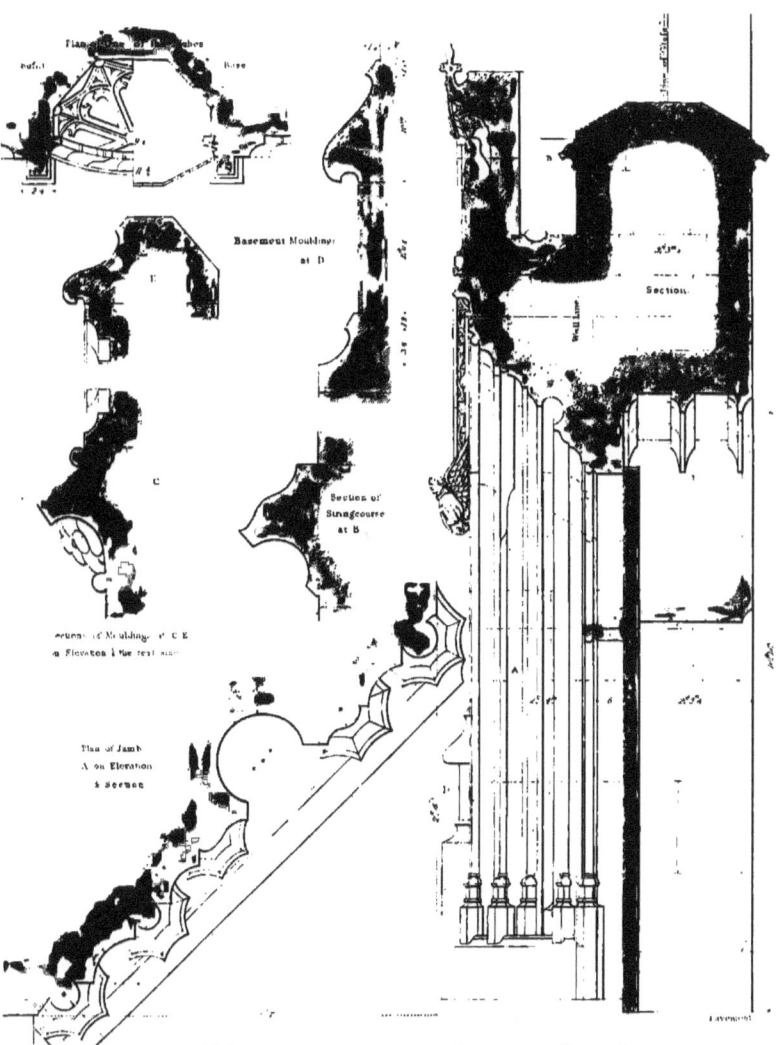

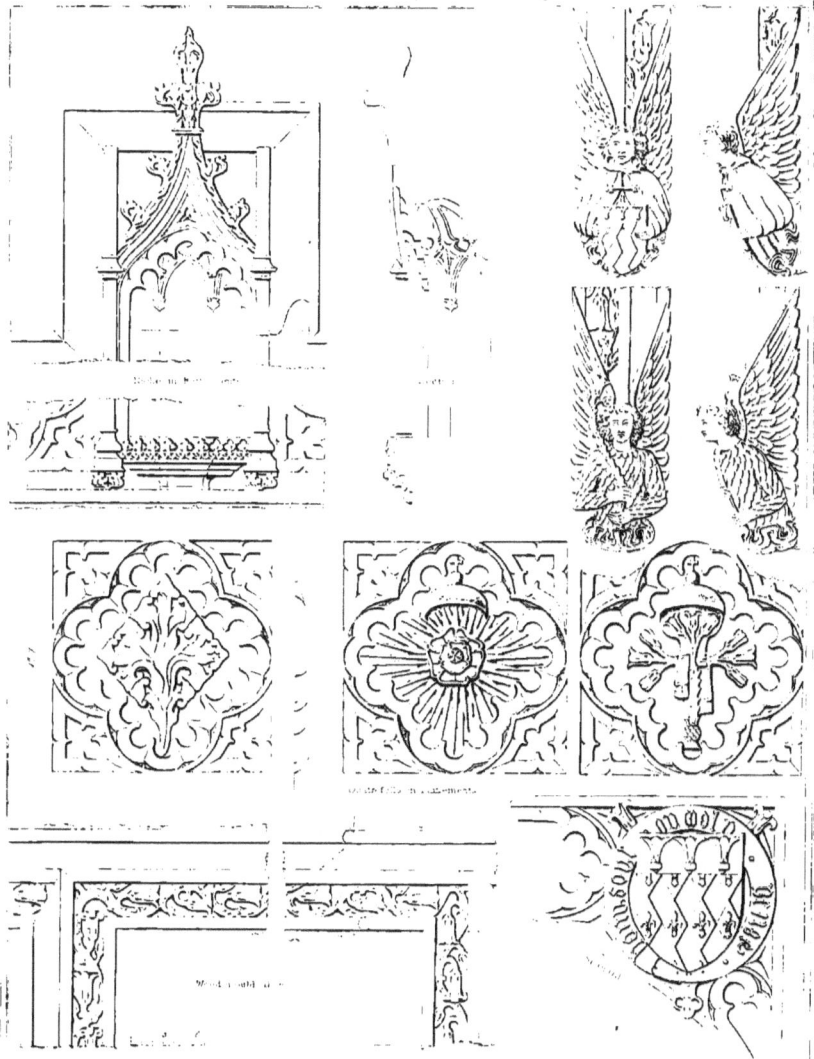

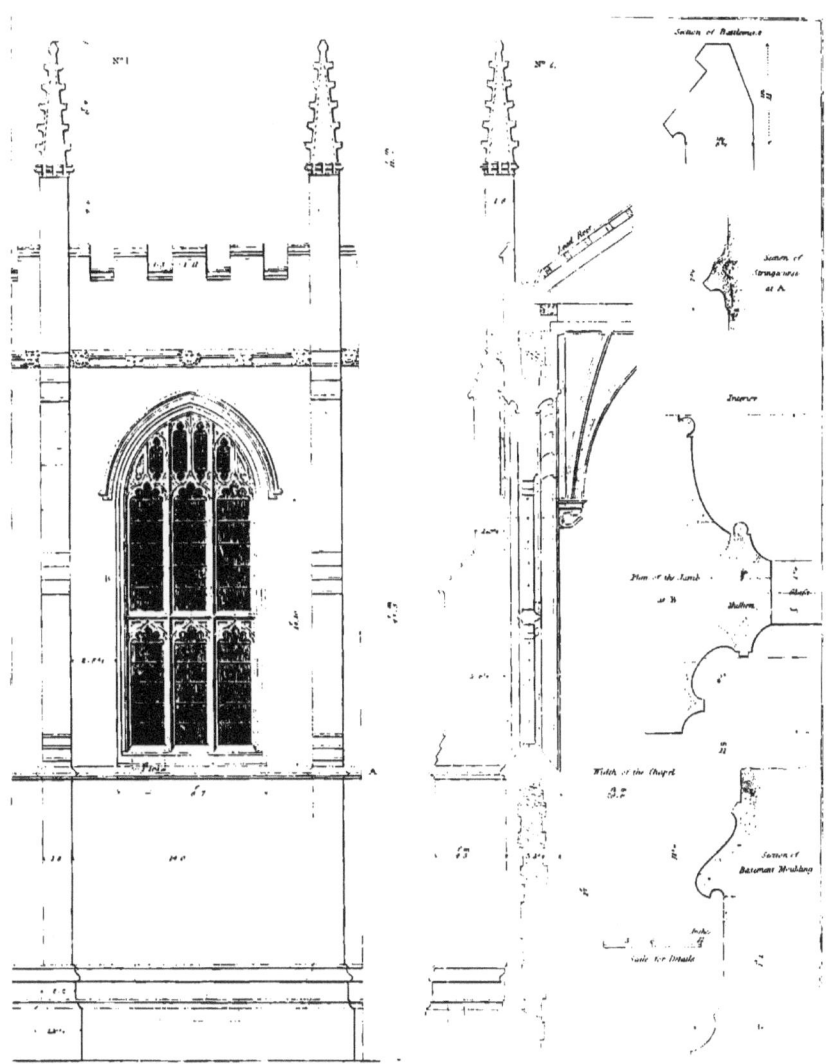

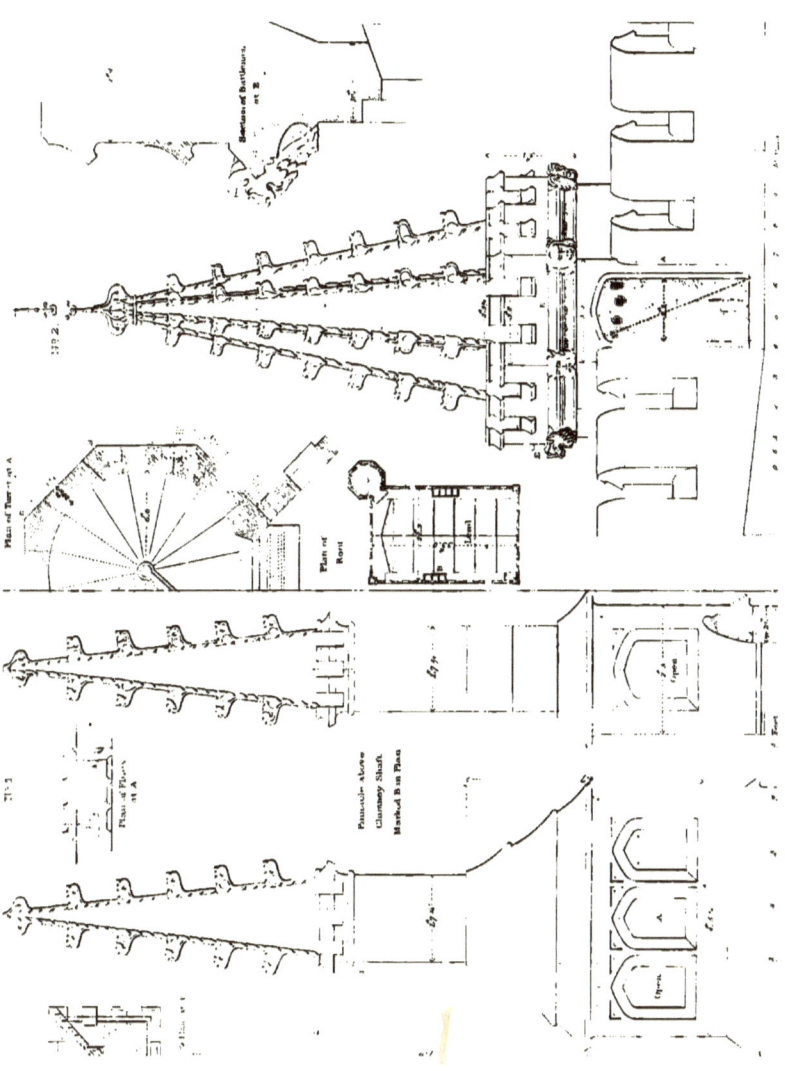

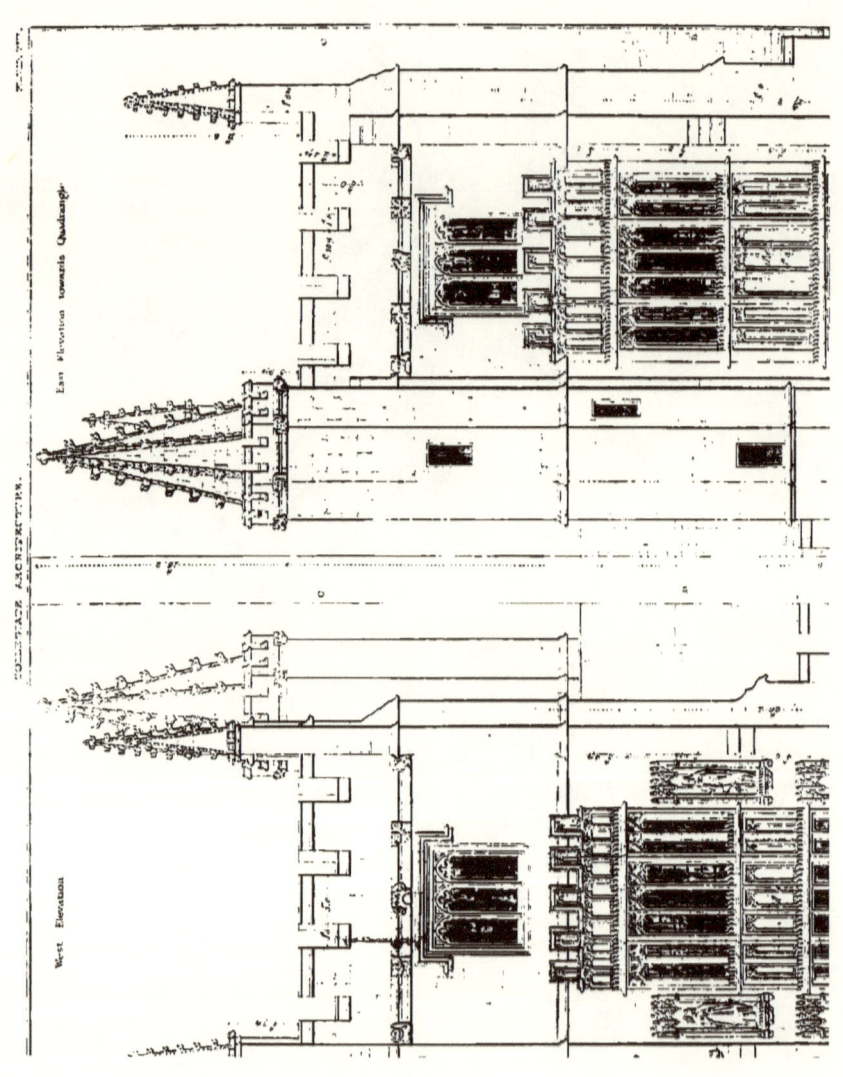

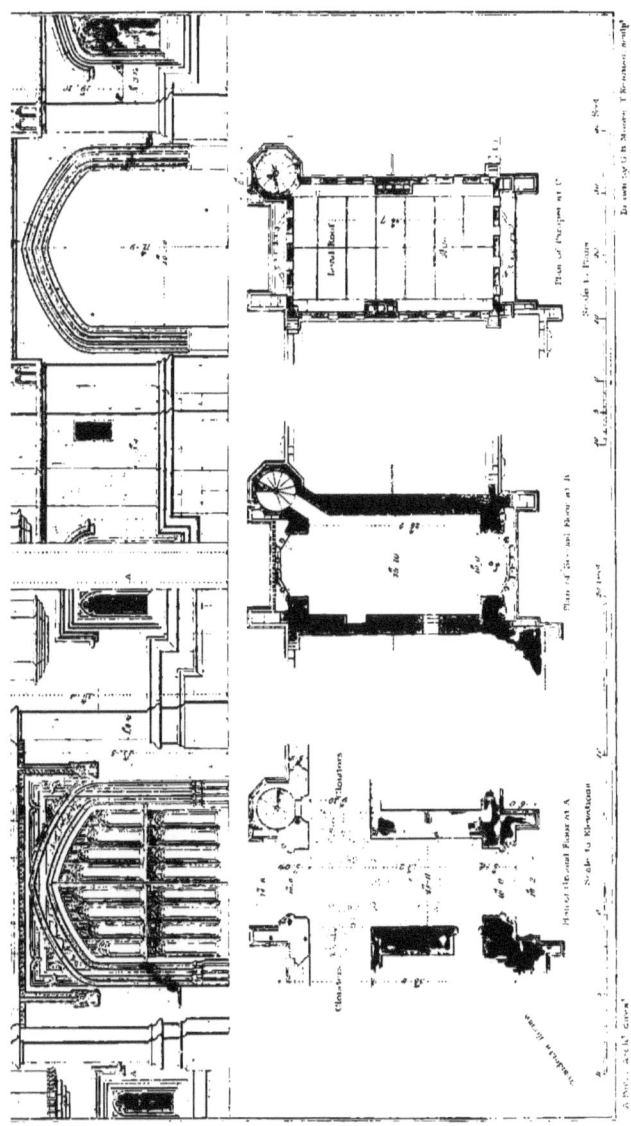

MAGDALENE COLLEGE, OXFORD.

Elevations and Plans of the Entrance leading to the Several Quadrangles

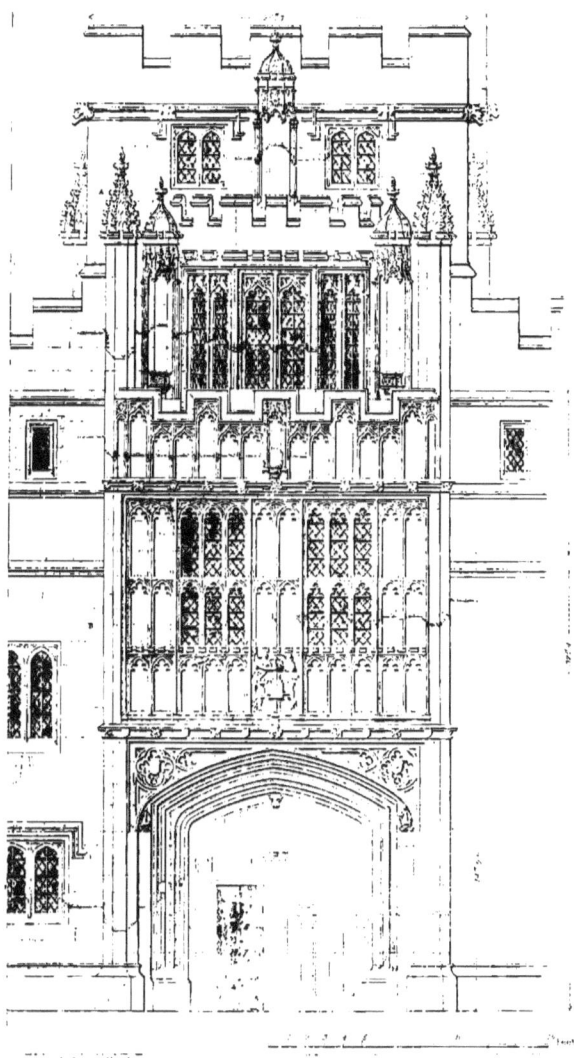

PORCH ON THE SOUTH SIDE

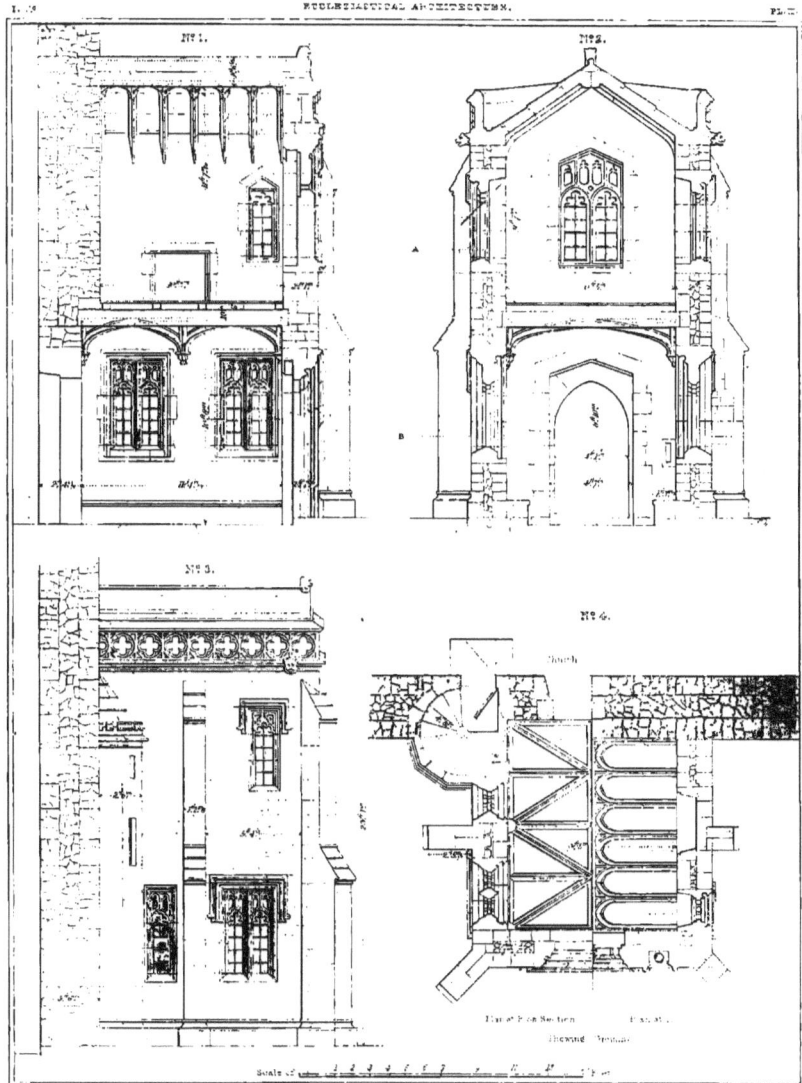

PORCH ON THE SOUTH SIDE OF
ST PETERS CHURCH OXFORD.

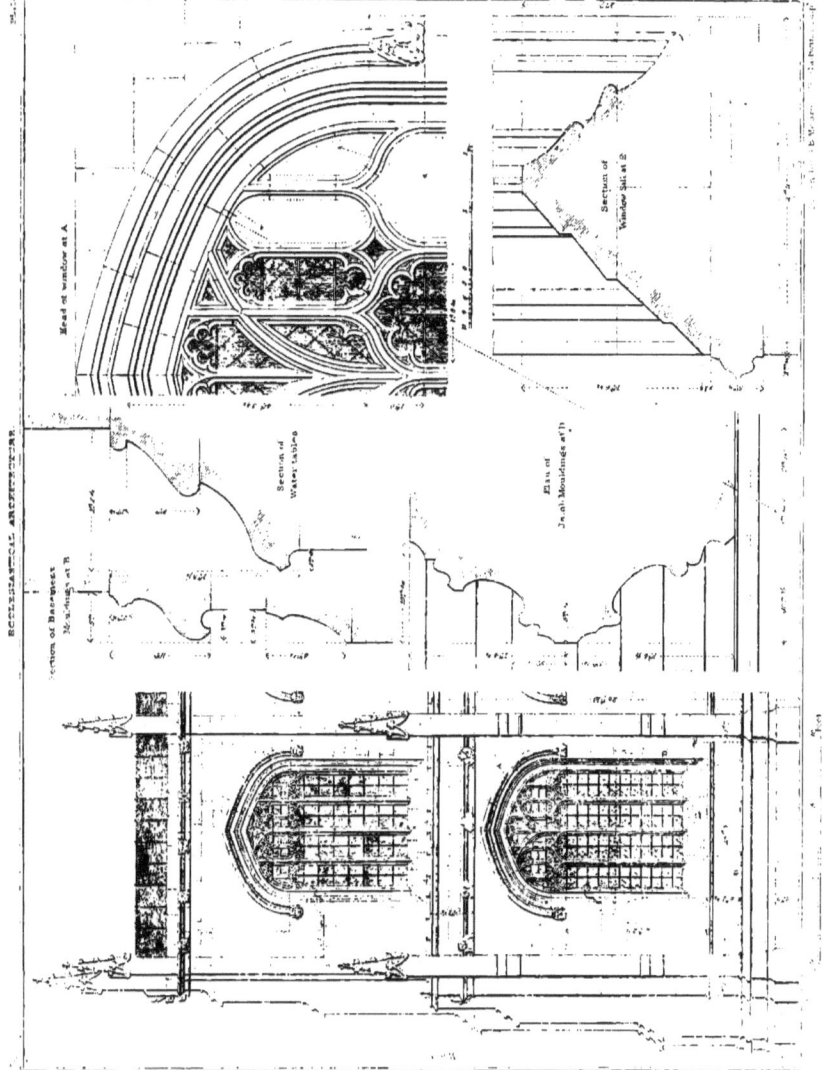

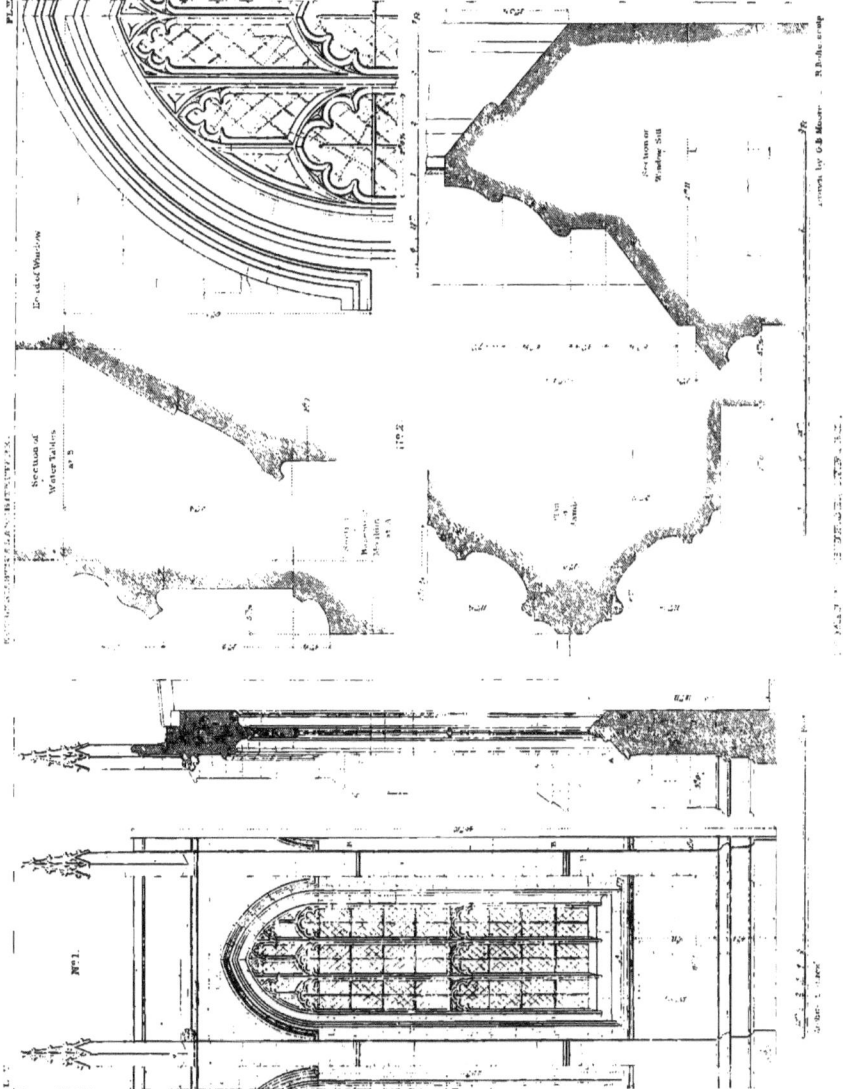

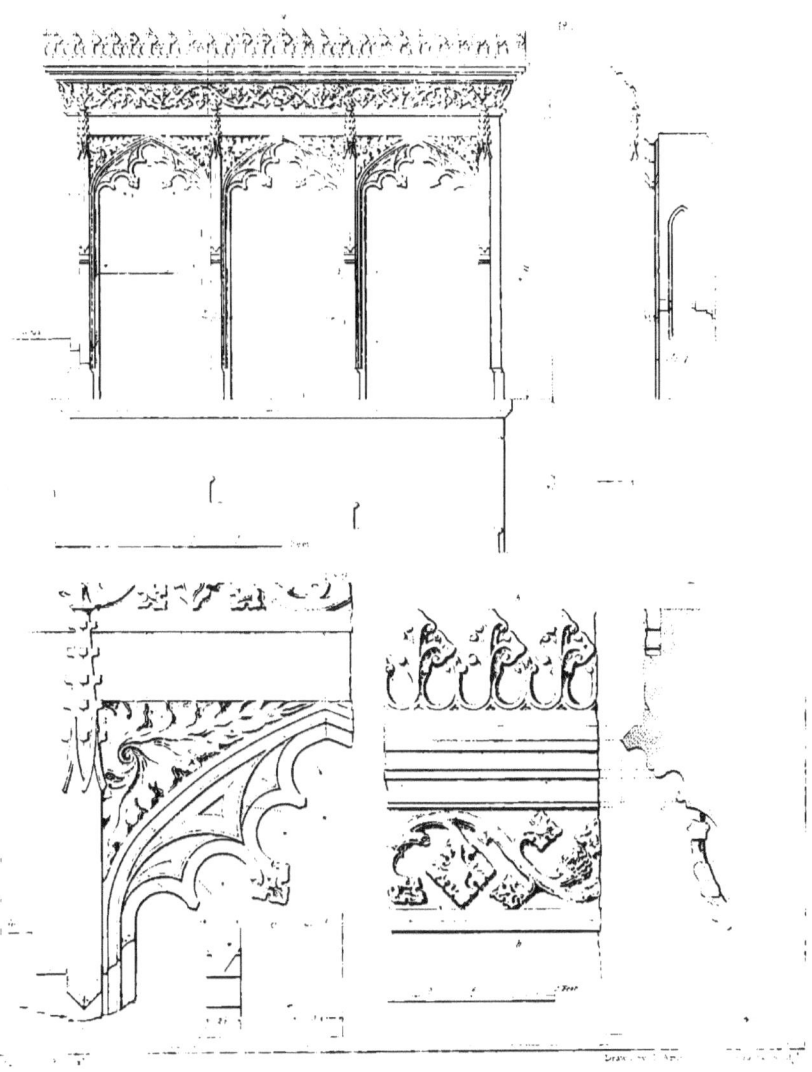

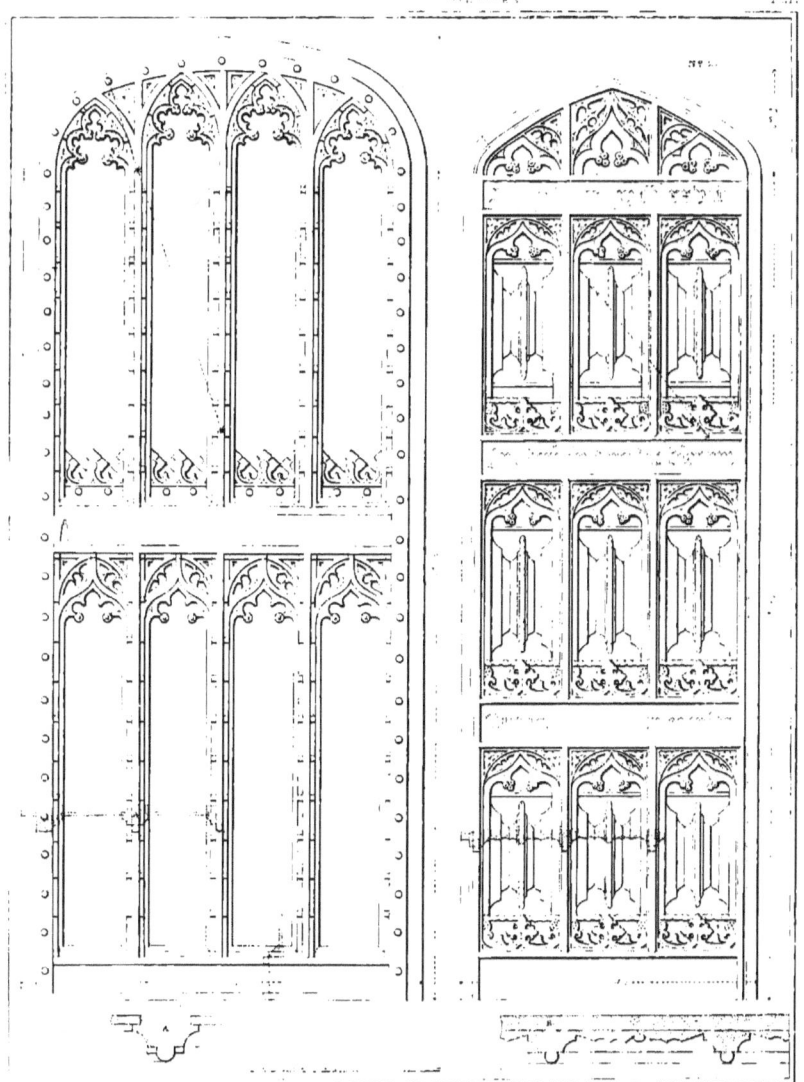

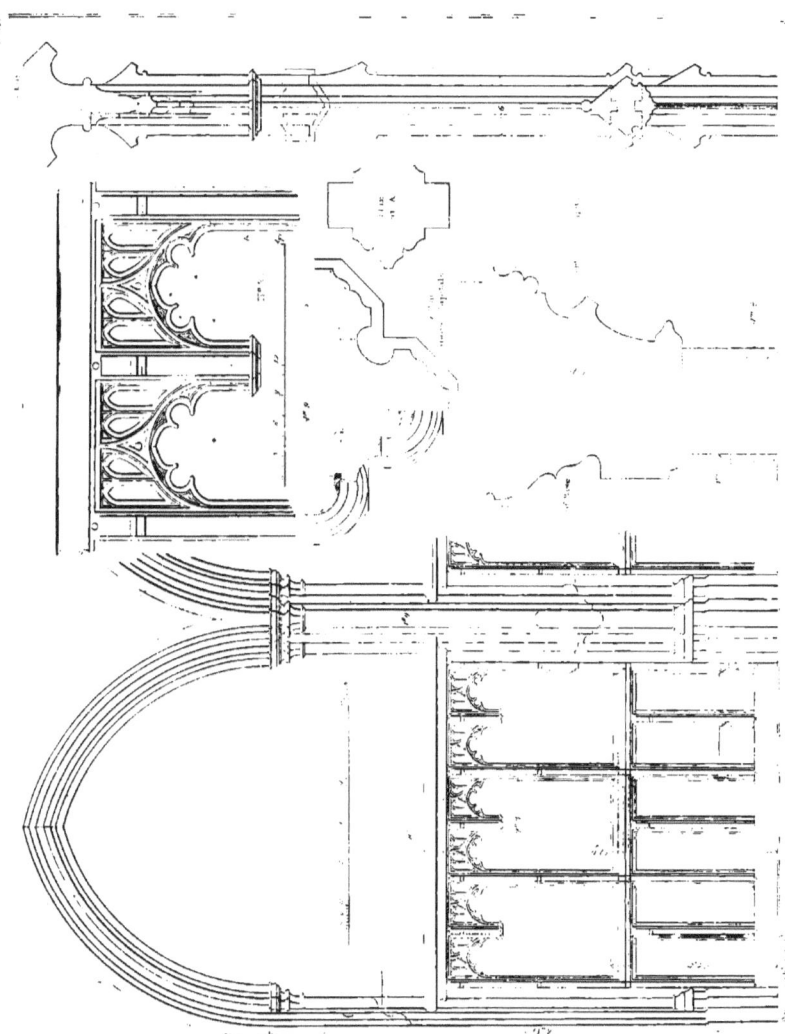

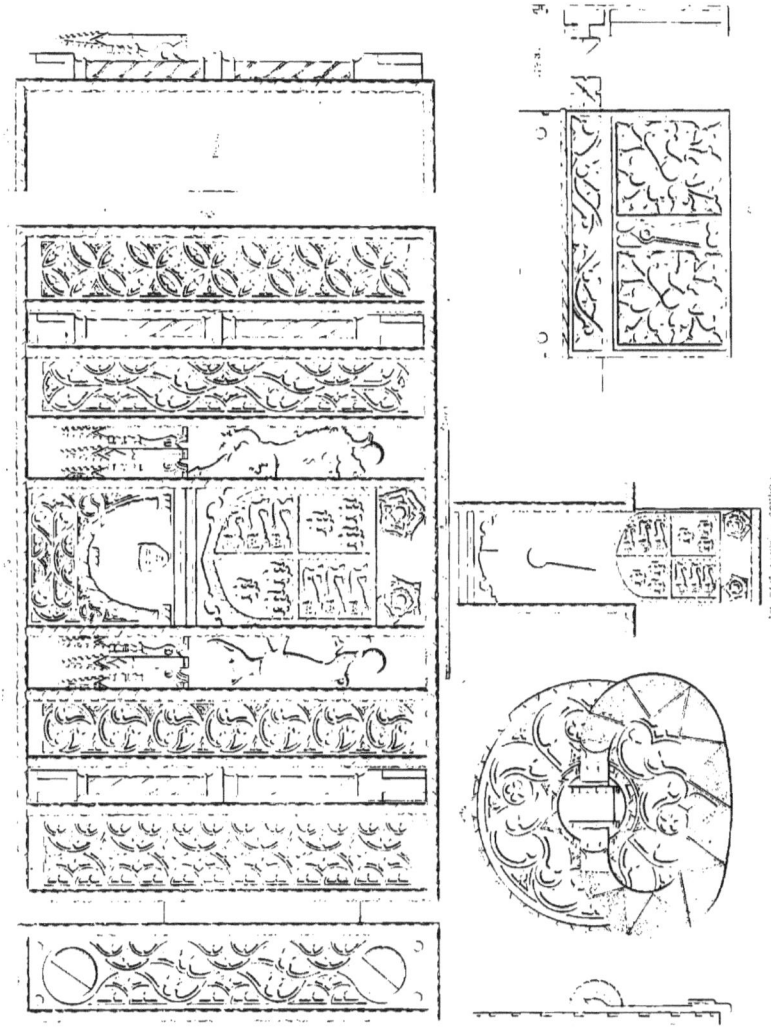

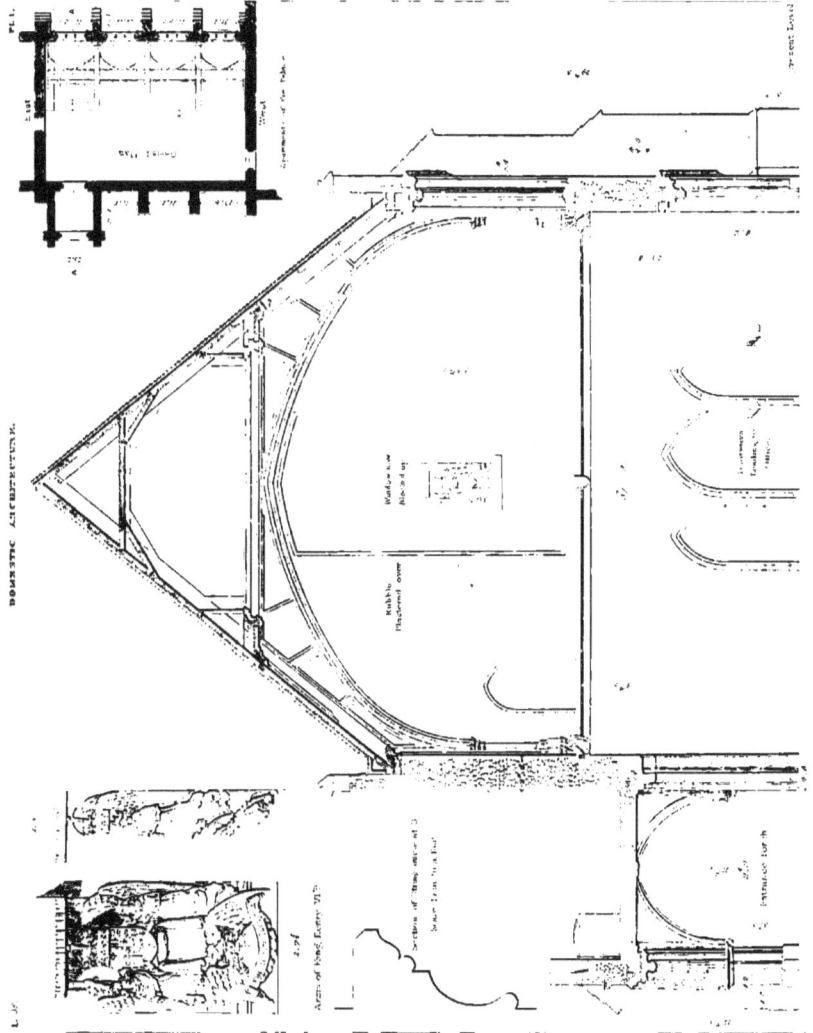

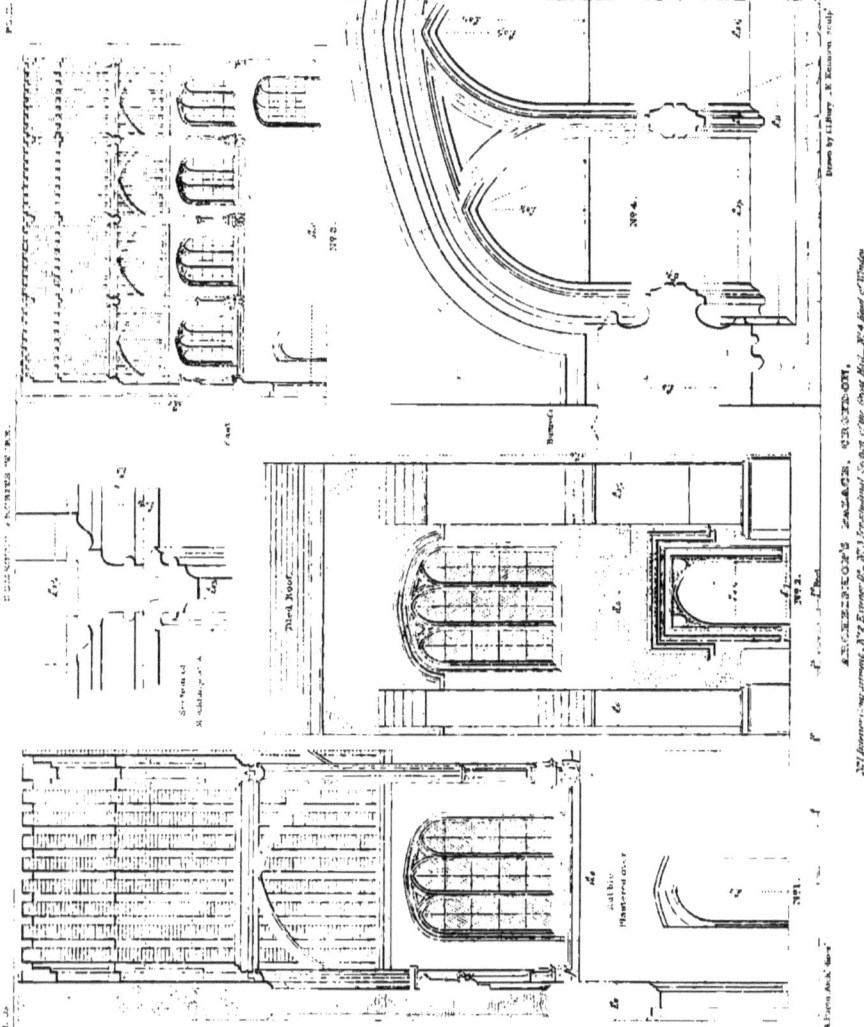

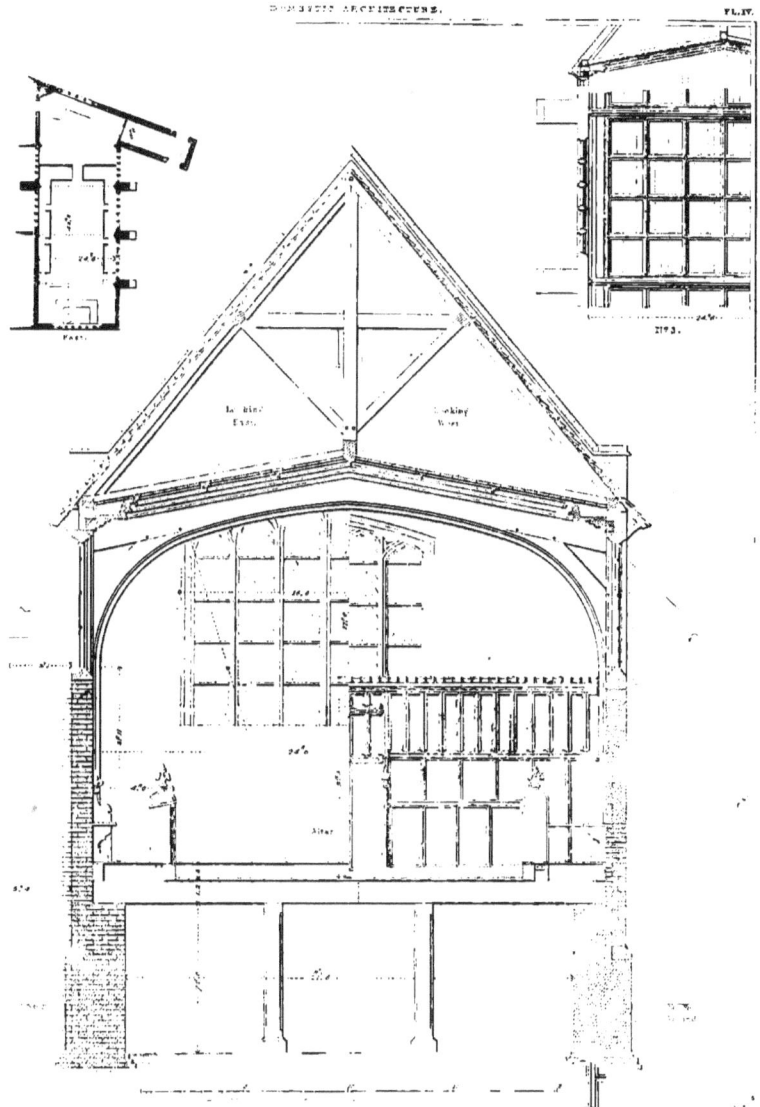

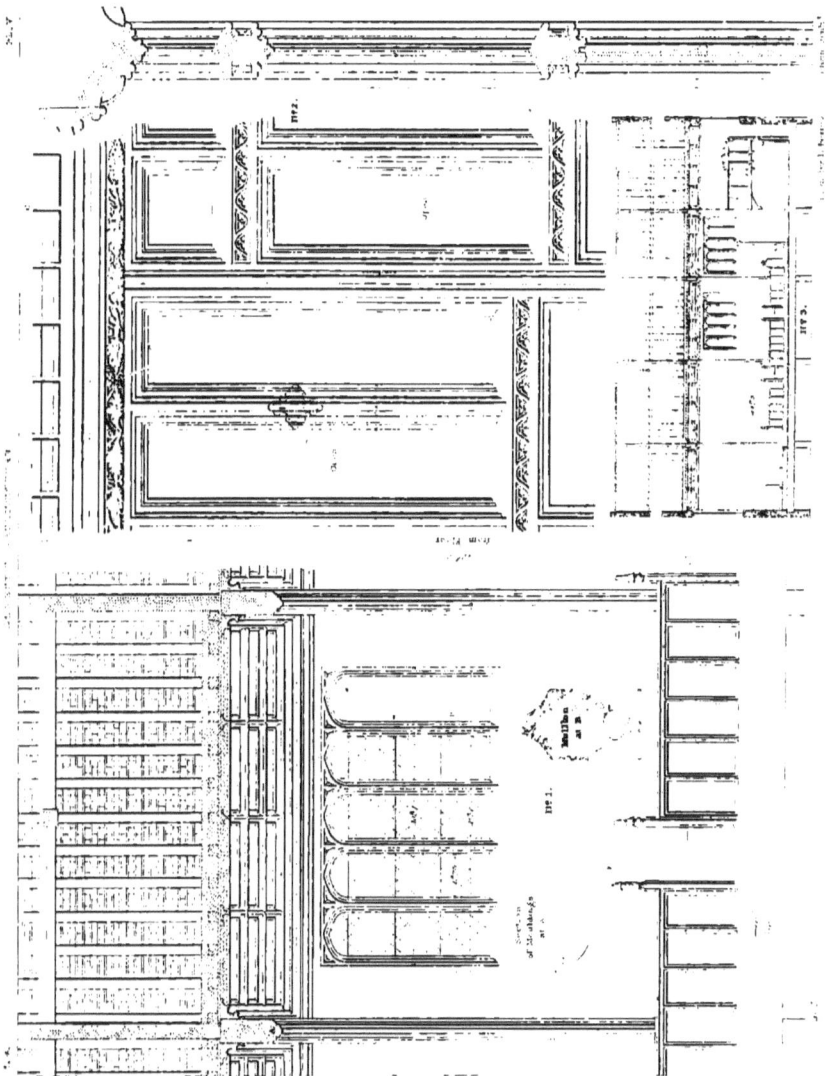

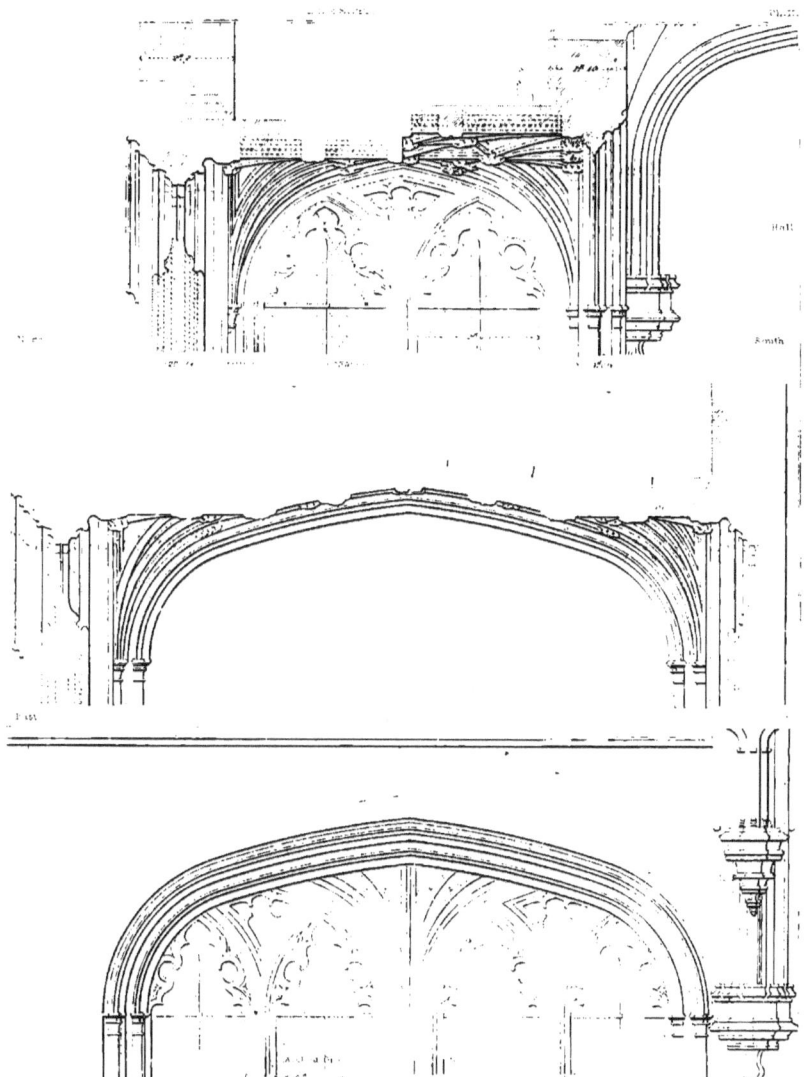

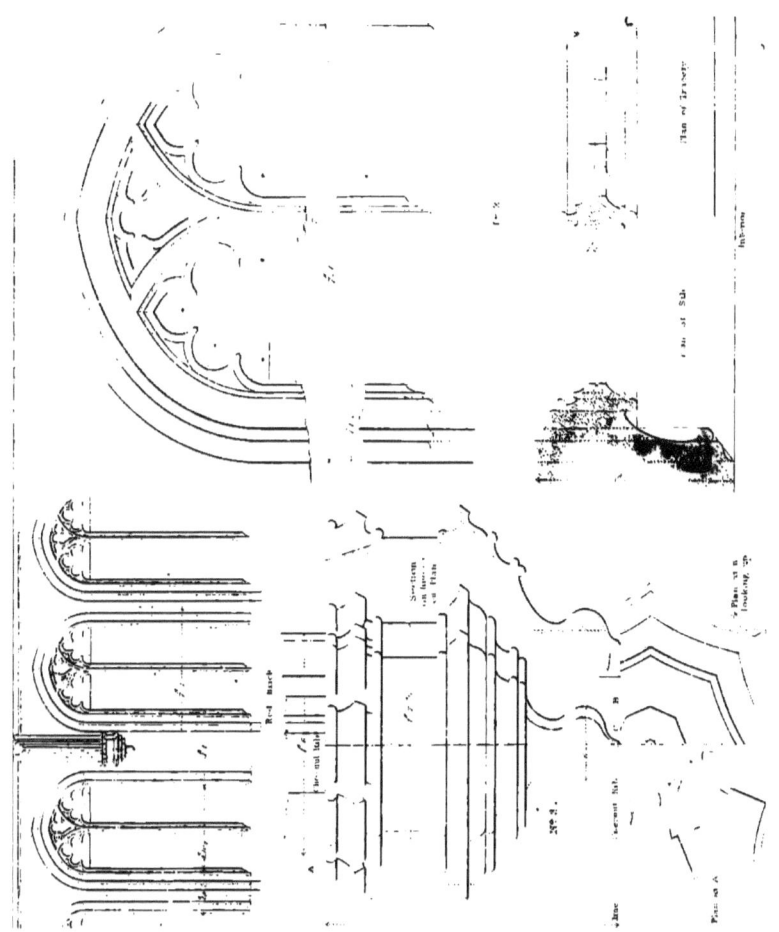

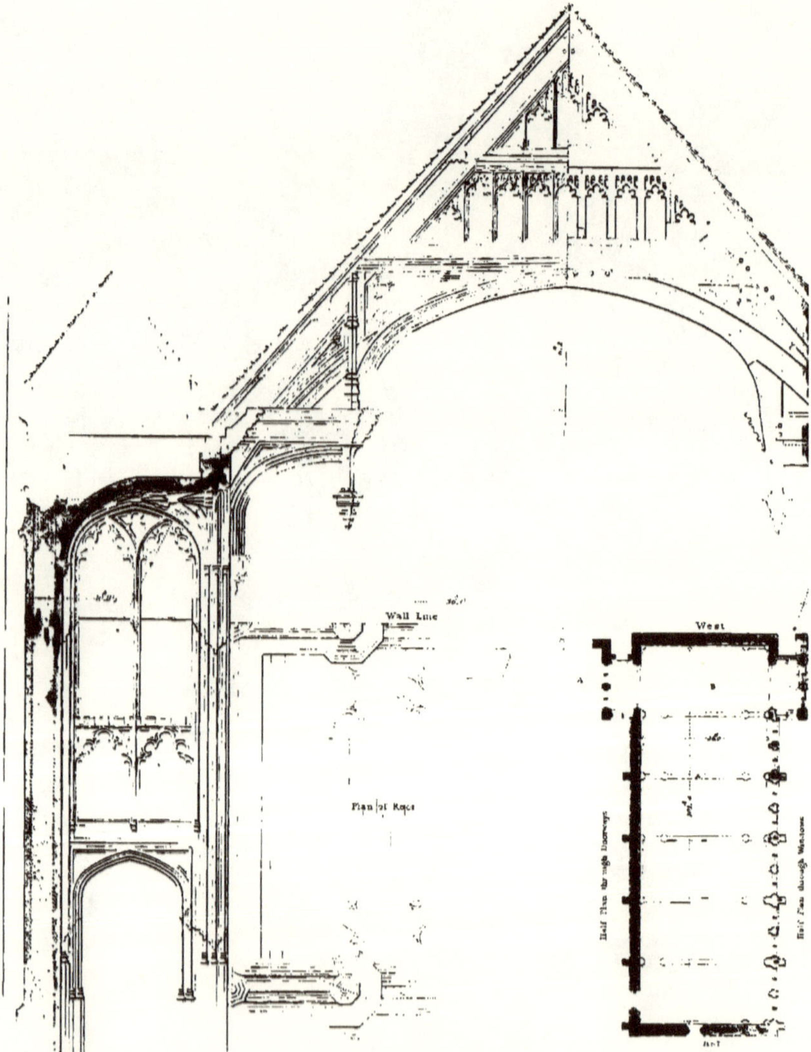

DOMESTIC A.

Wall Line

West

Plan of Roof

Half Plan through Doorway

Half Plan through Windows

A Pugin. Arch.t direx.t

Foot

Drawn by I.T.Bury — Gladwin sculp.

CE, KENT.

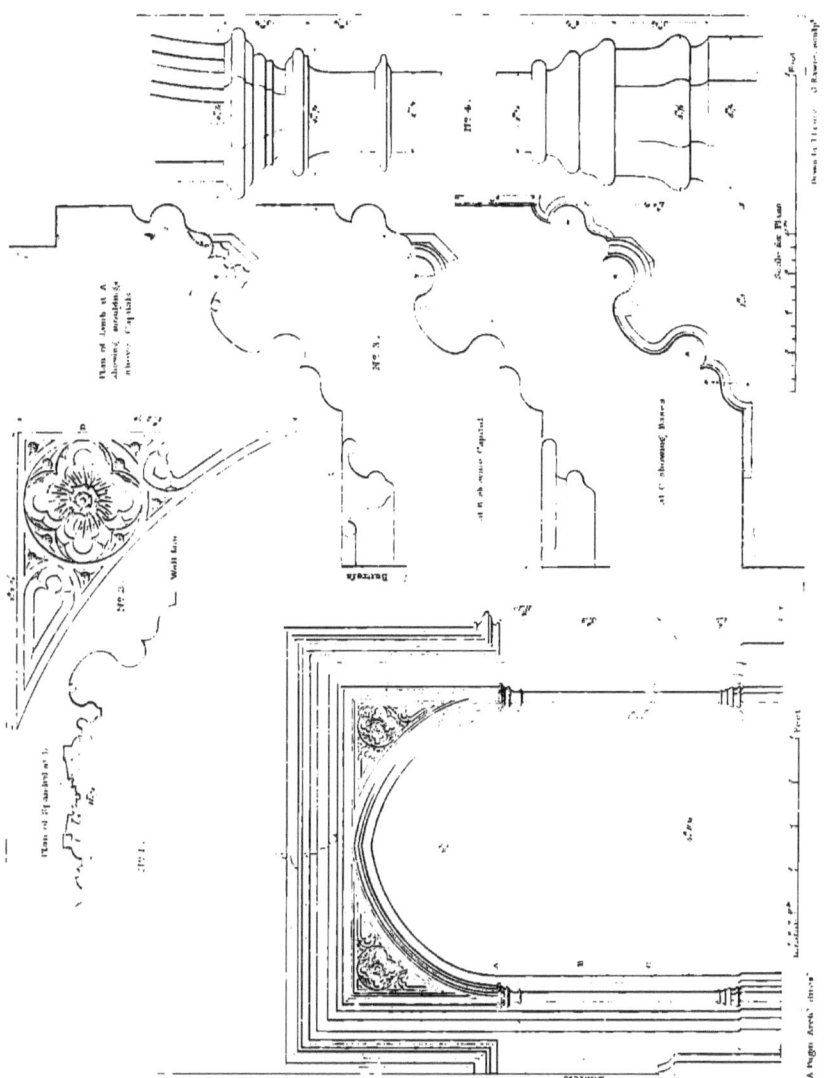

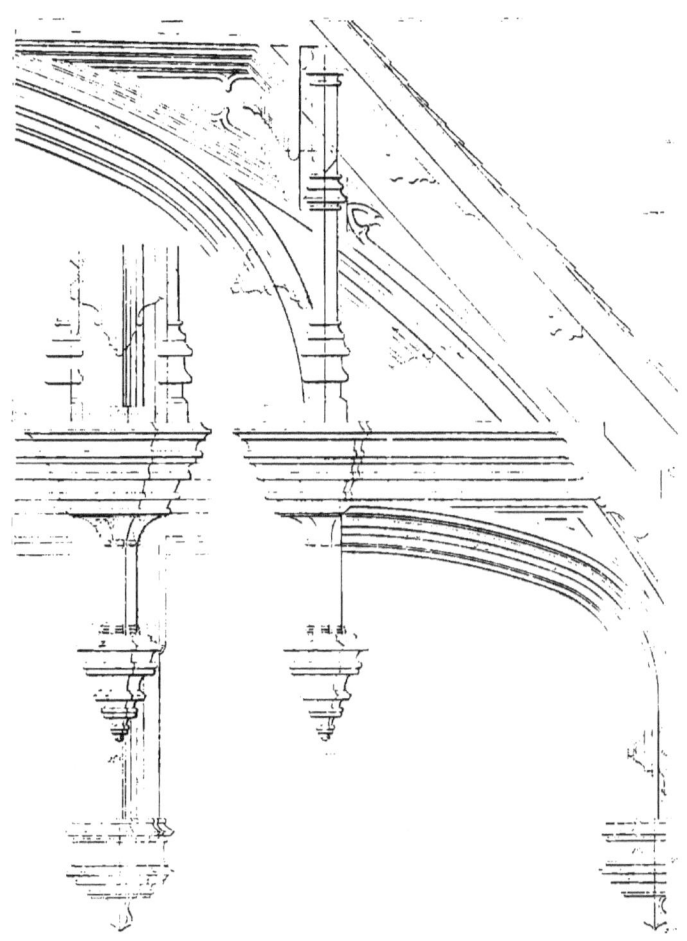

Plan showing General Arrangement

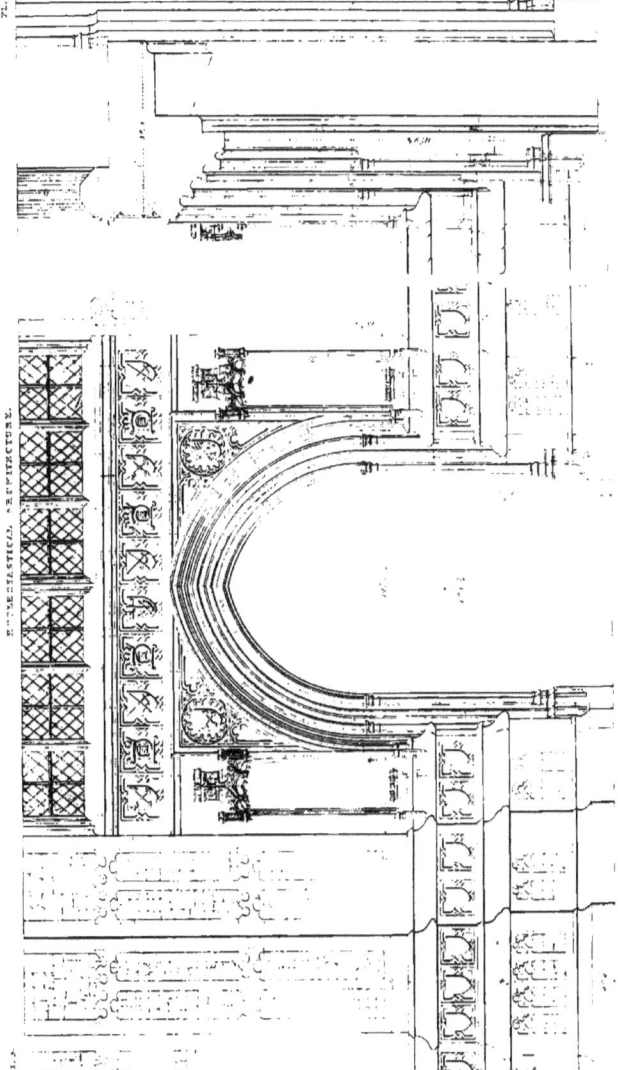

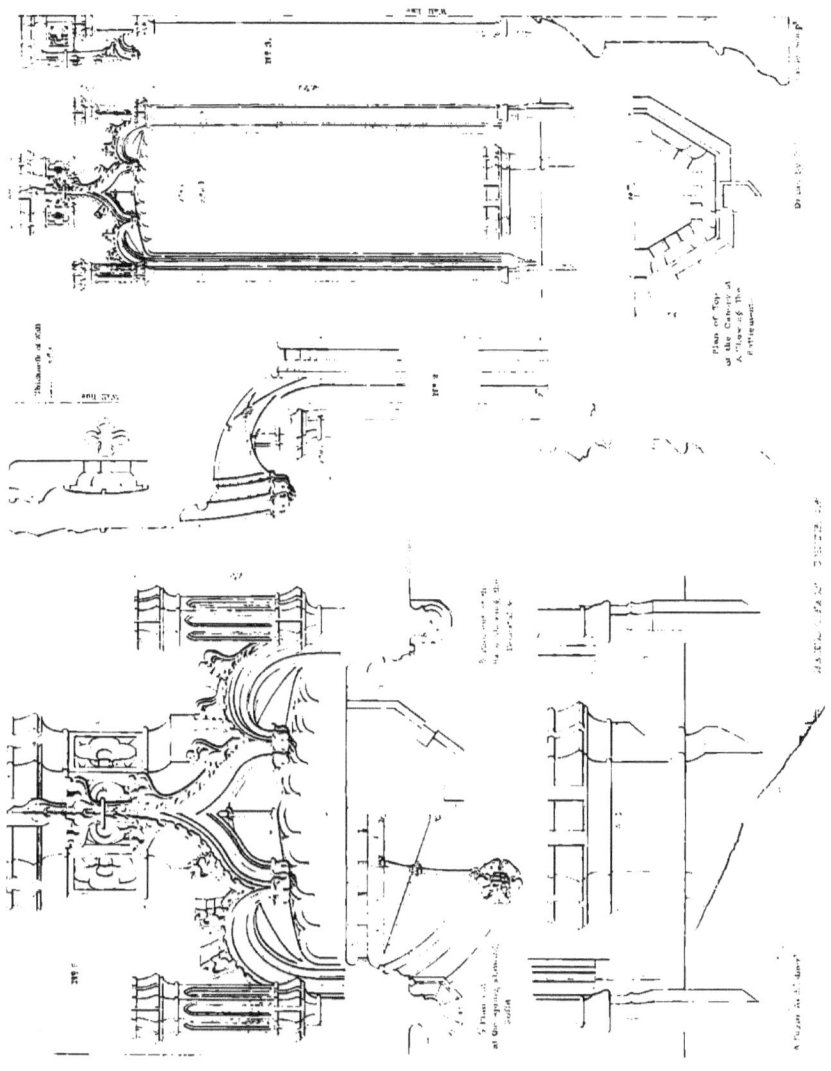

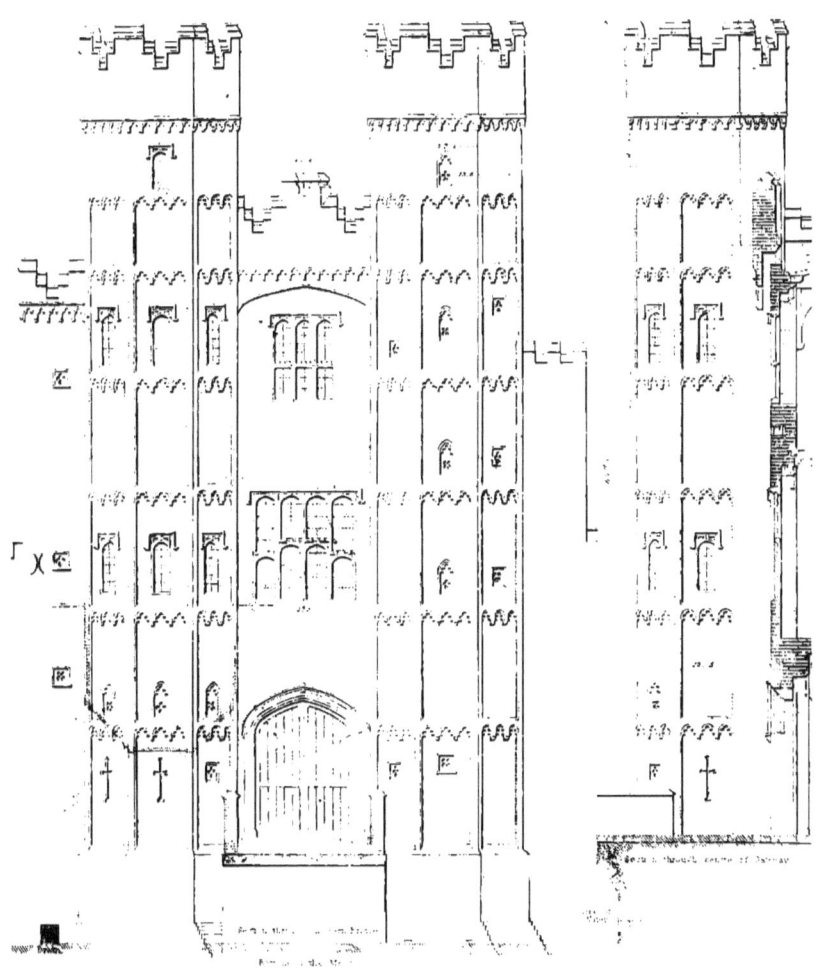

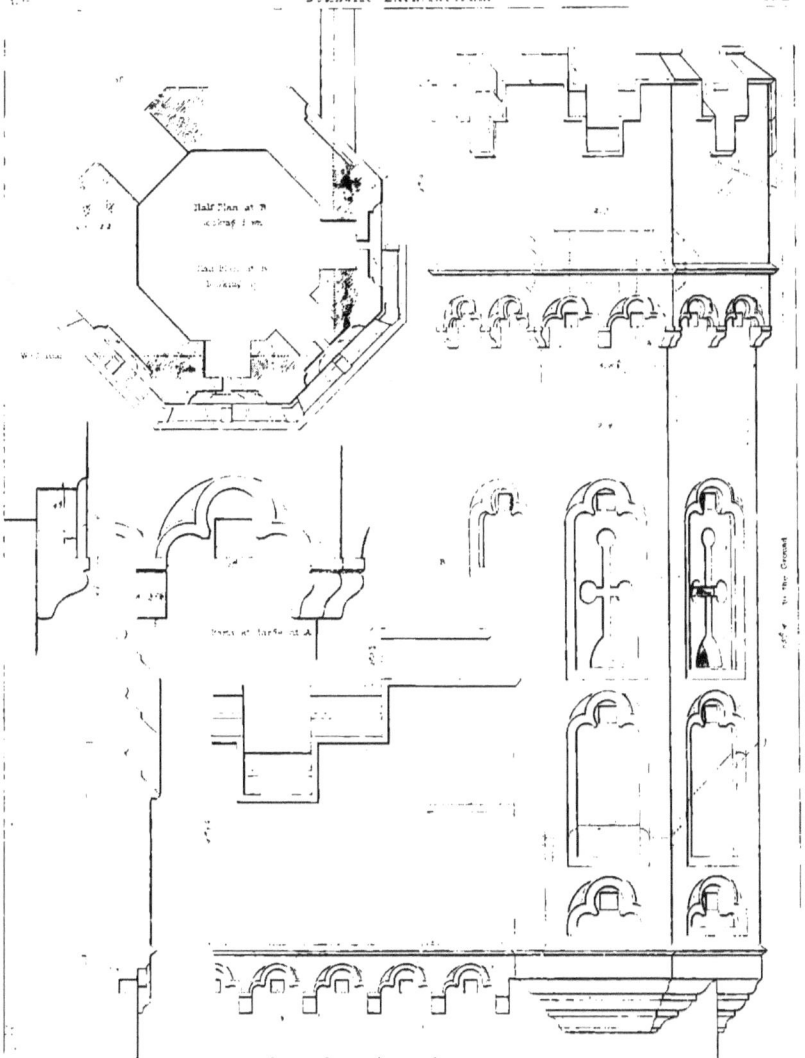

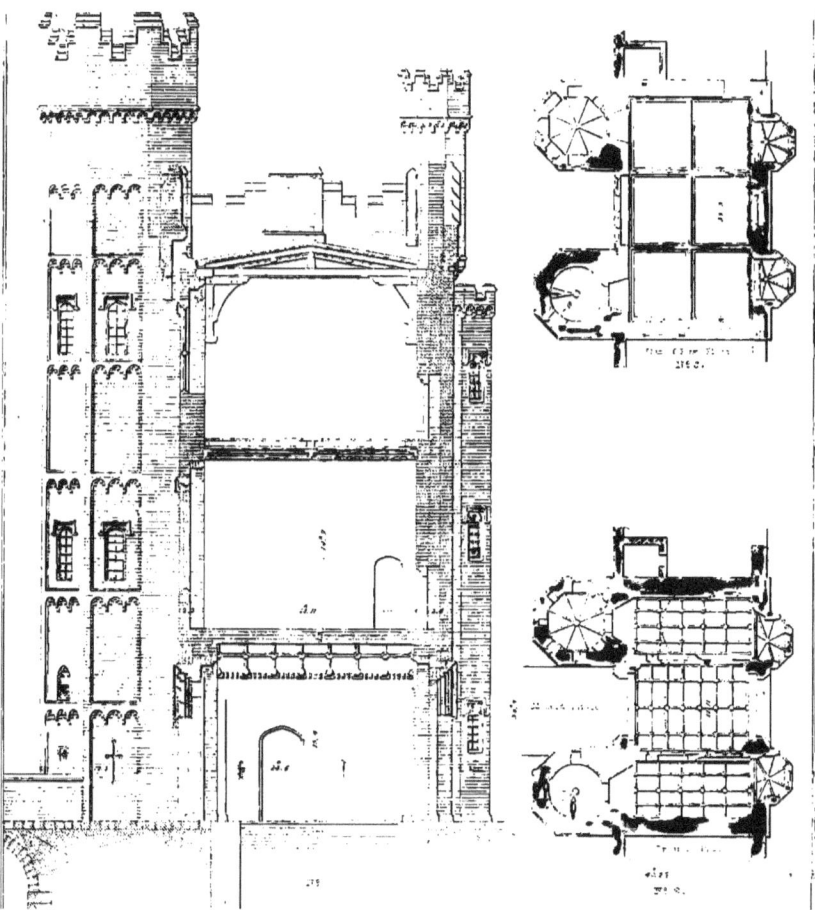

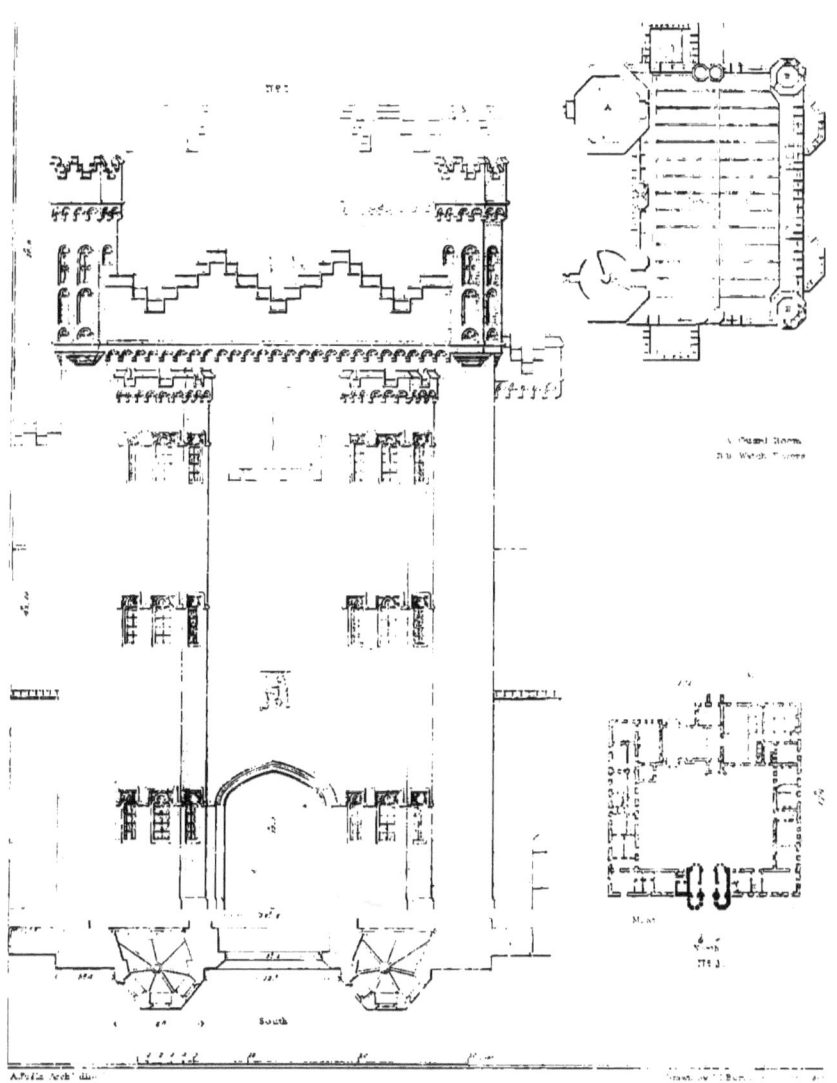

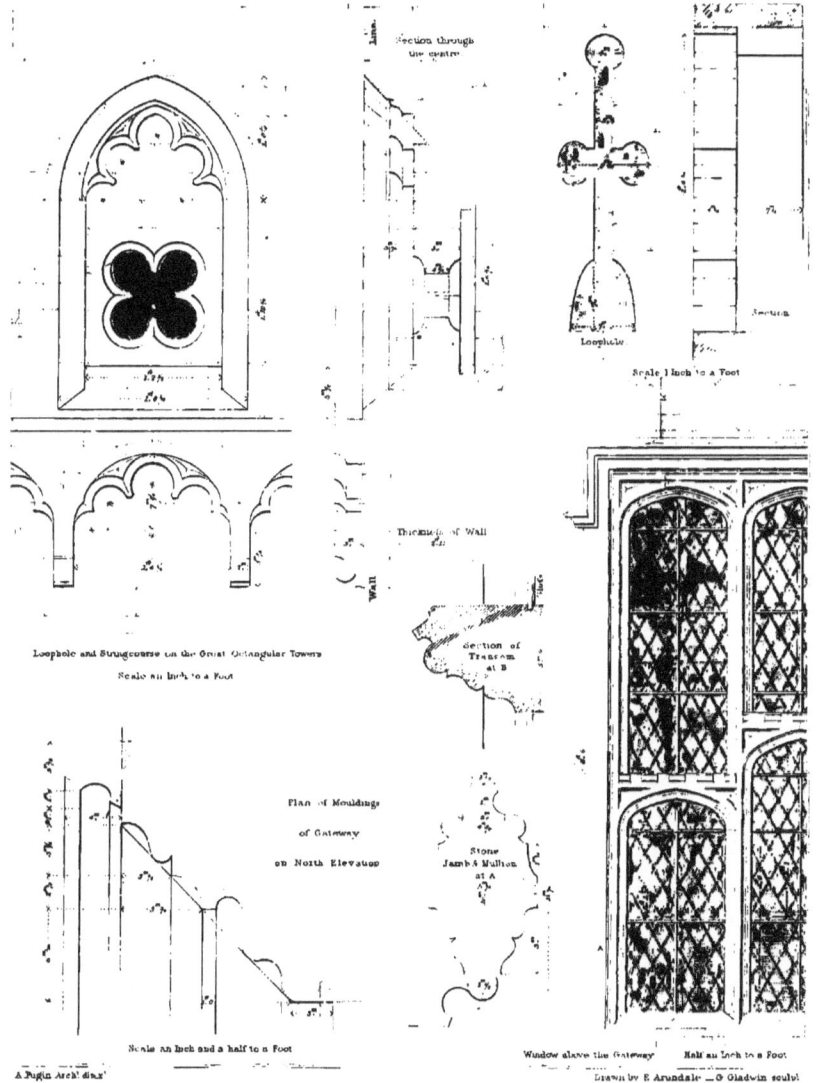

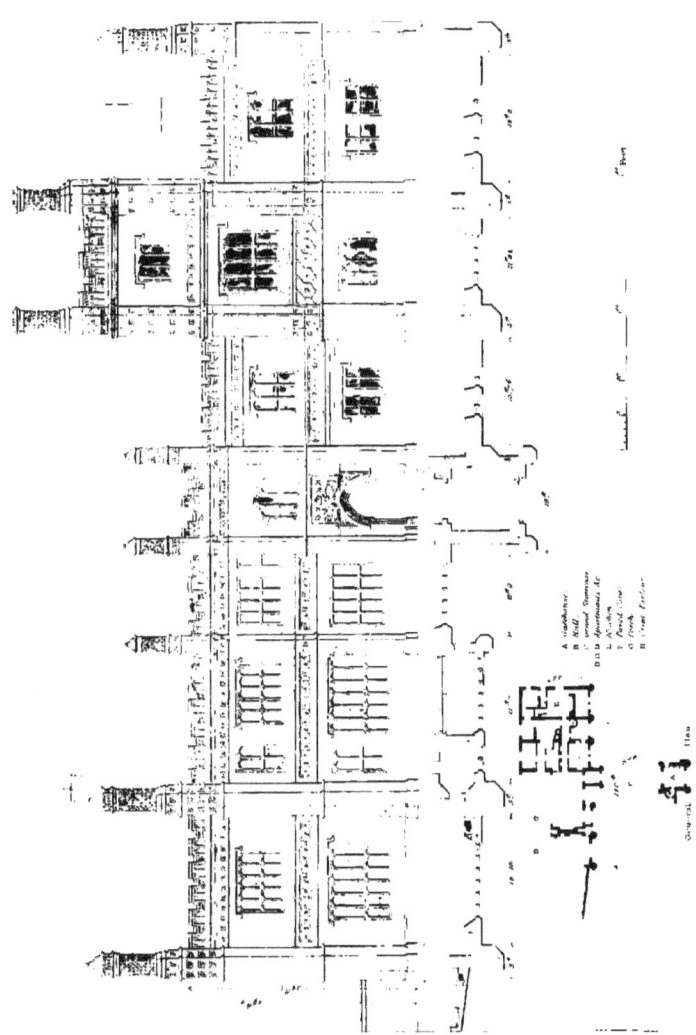

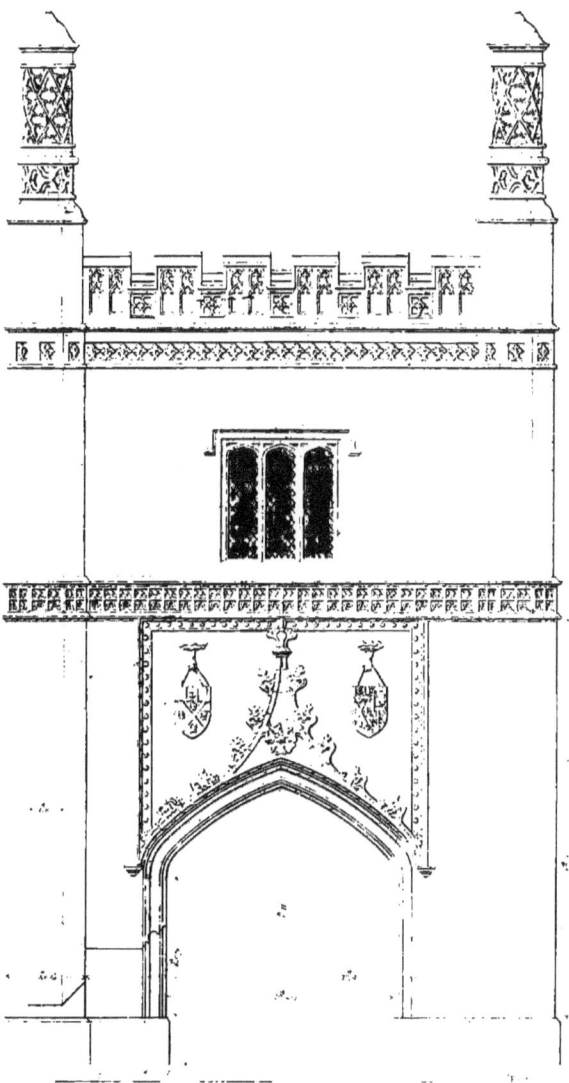

MANOR HOUSE EAST BARSHAM.
Elevation and Section of Tower South Front

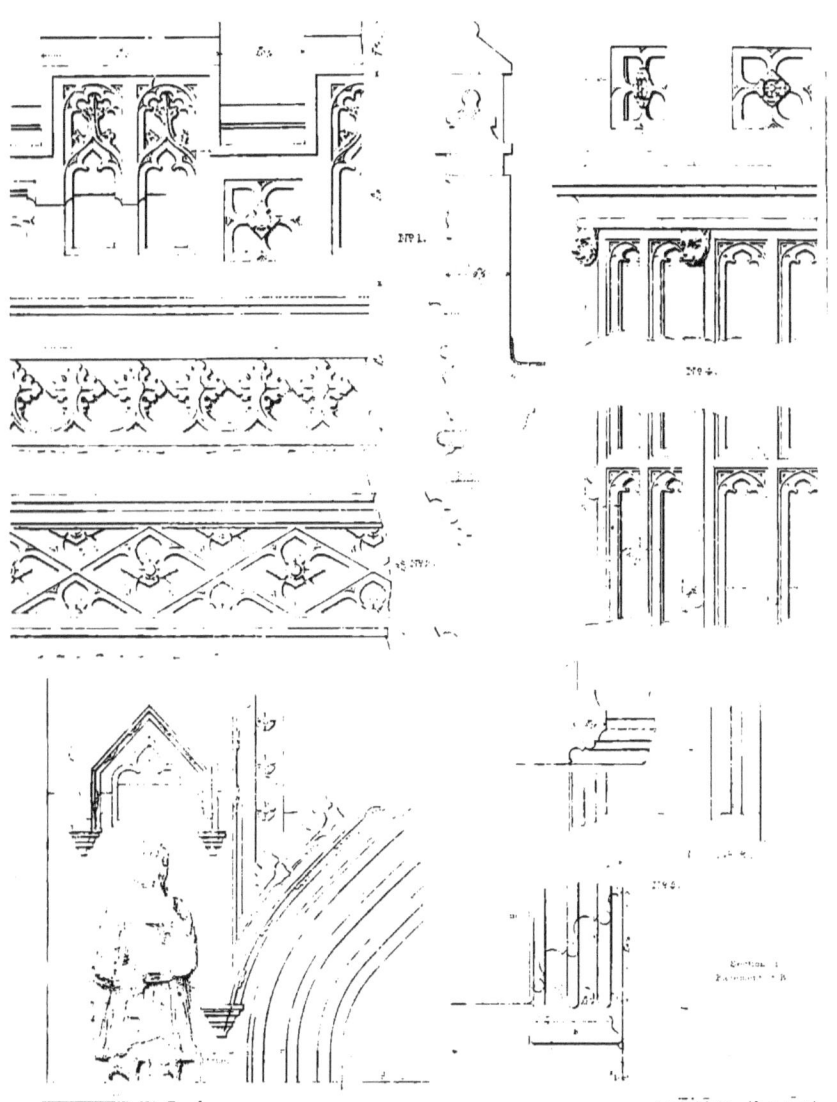

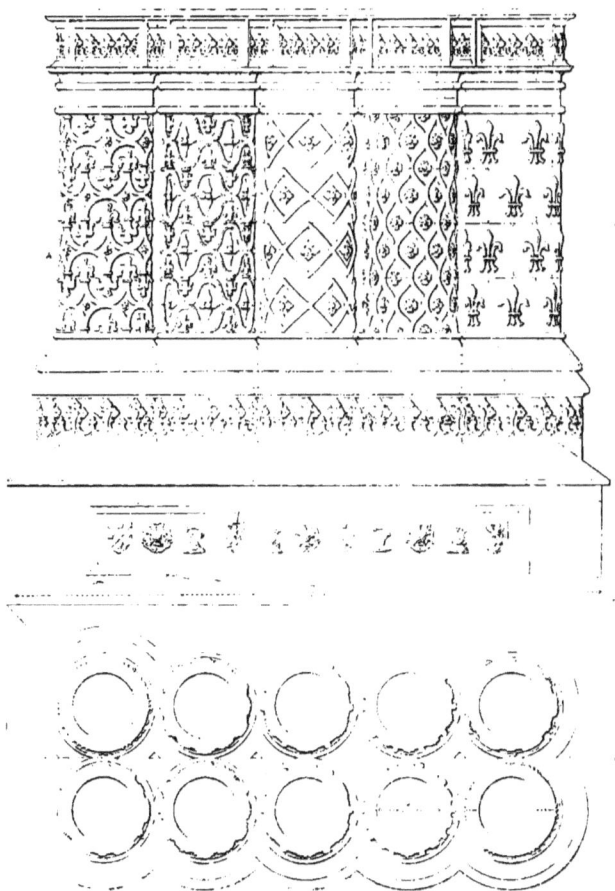

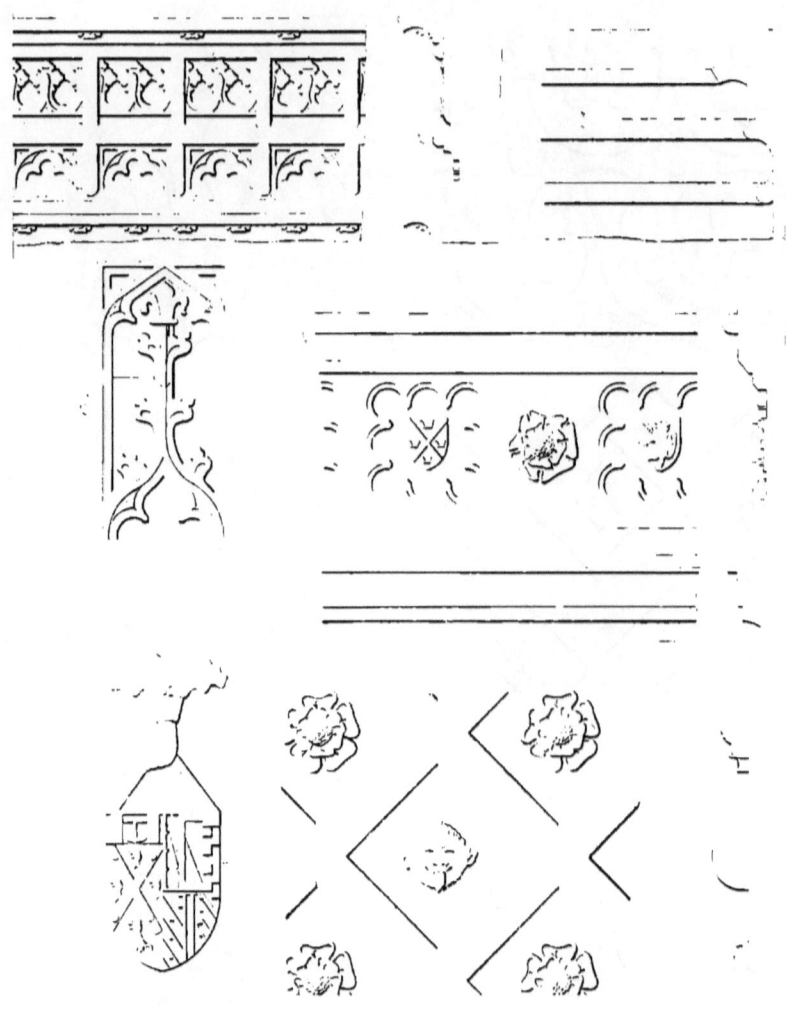

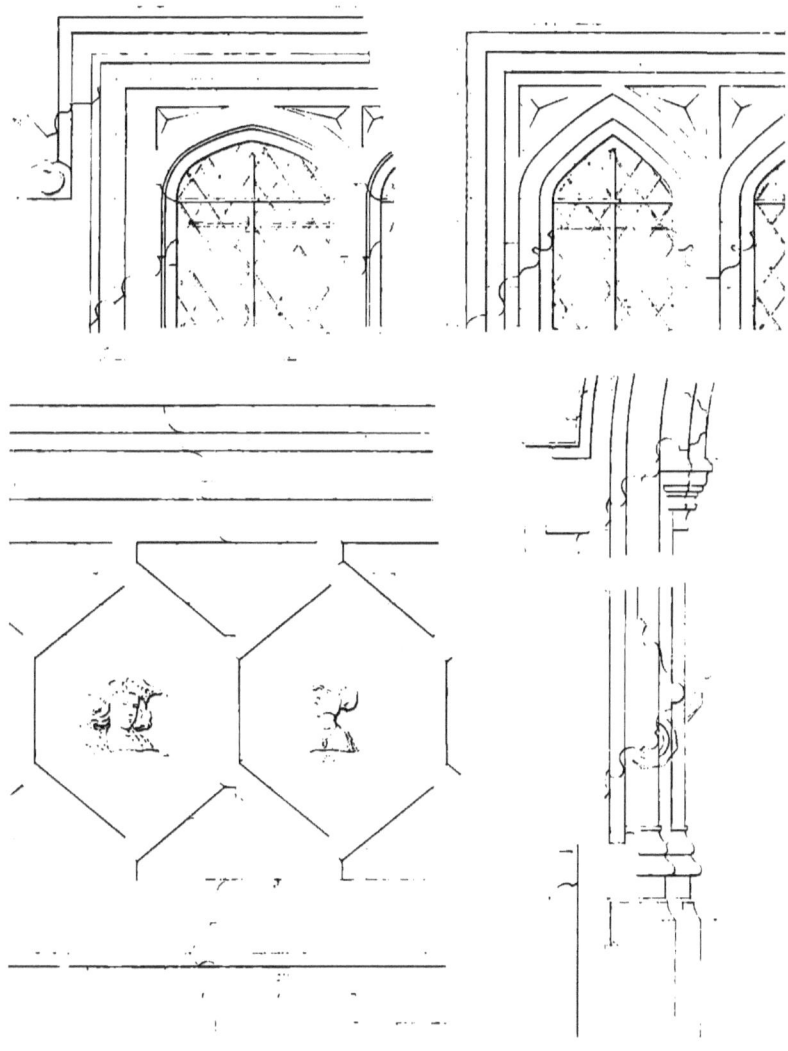

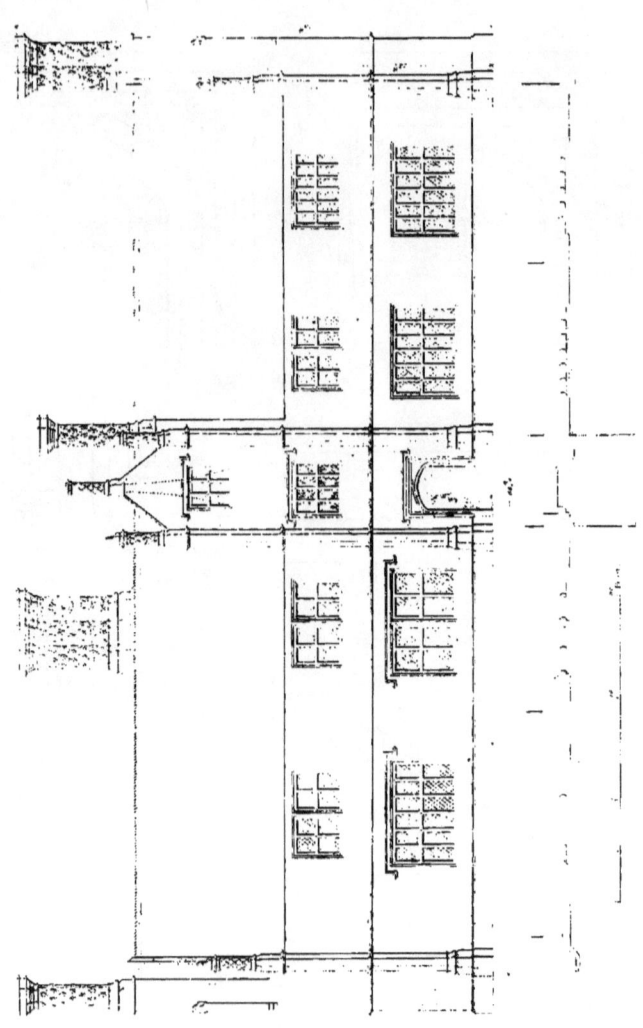

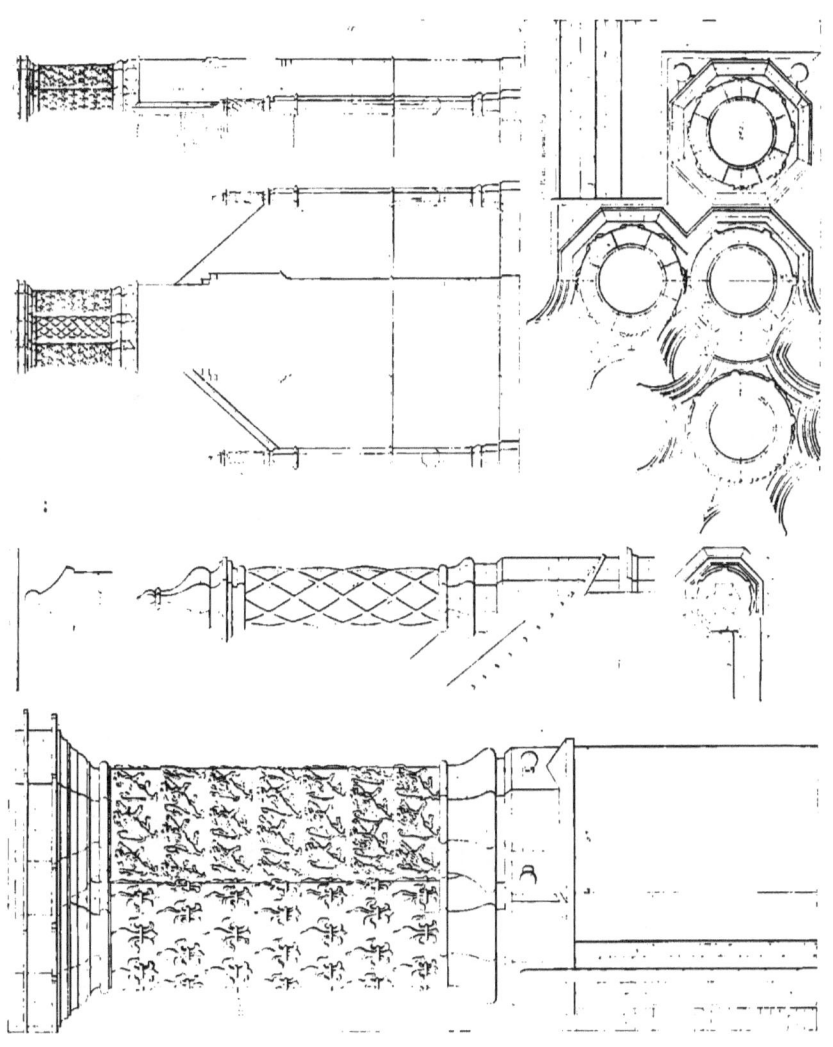

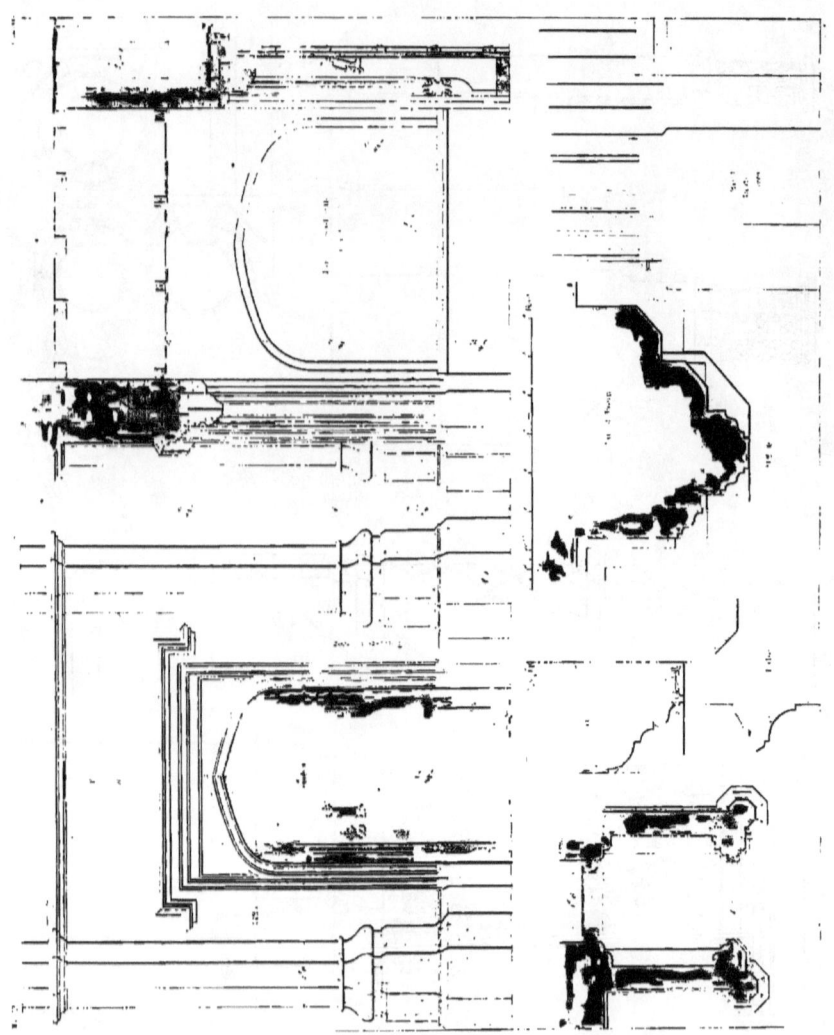

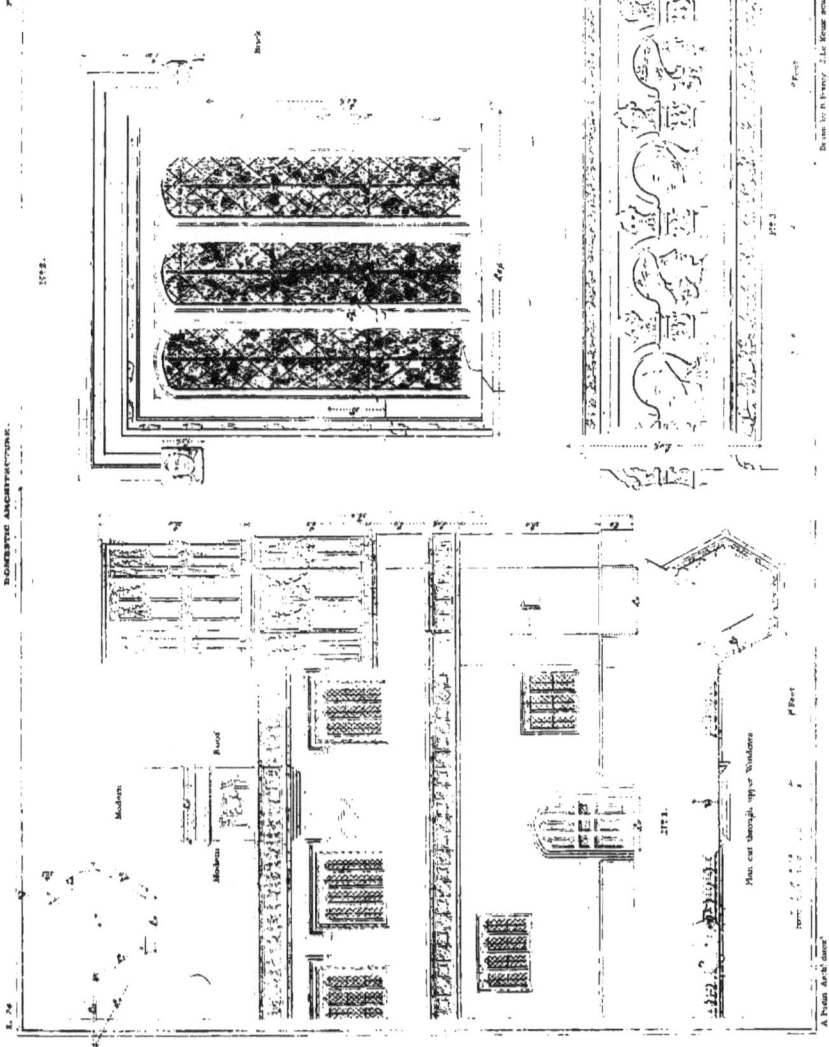

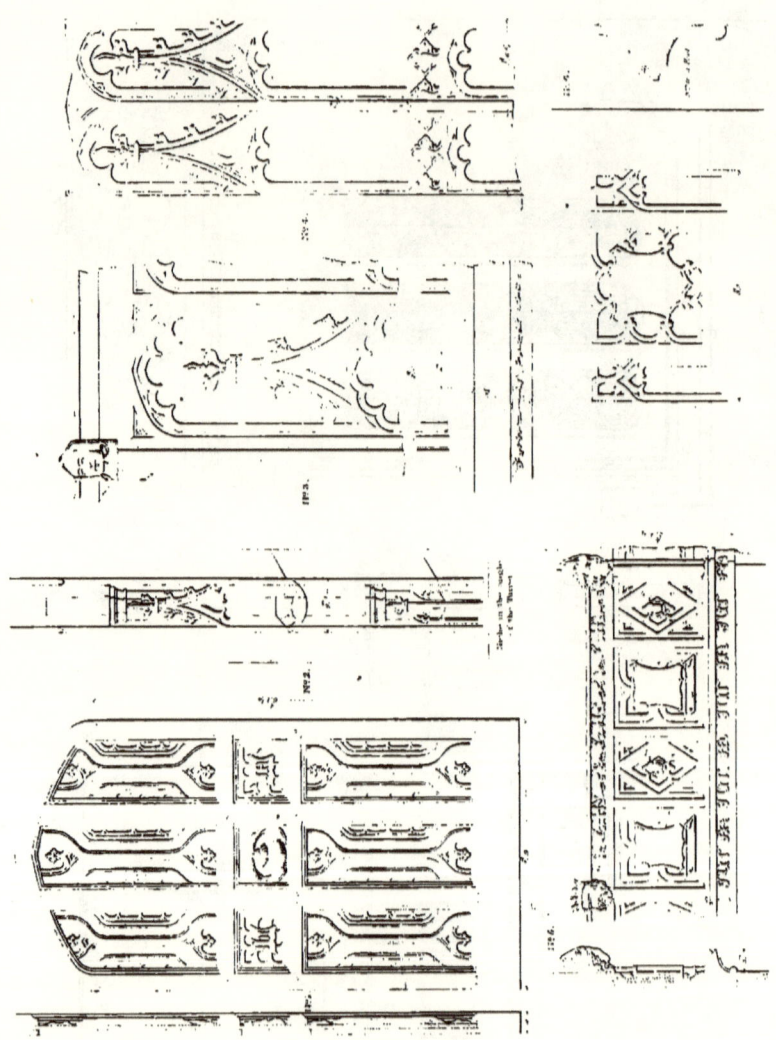

www.ingramcontent.com/pod-product-compliance
Lightning Source LLC
Chambersburg PA
CBHW021013240426
43669CB00037B/1047